F.R. Ray ♡

There's Power In Your Tongue

Praise God ♡

Elissa

There's Power In Your Tongue

Maria Vadia

Queenship

PUBLISHING COMPANY
P.O. Box 220 • Goleta, CA 93116
(800) 647-9882 • (805) 692-0043 • Fax: (805) 967-5133

About the author, **Maria Vadia**

Born in Havana, Cuba, Maria was 10 years old when she and her family fled to Miami, Florida to escape the communist regime in her native country. She attended Catholic schools and was a "Sunday" Catholic with no personal relationship with the Lord Jesus Christ. Later married to a wealthy man, she was gripped by materialism; yet in the midst of everything the world could offer, she knew that something was missing.

Maria was baptized in the Holy Spirit in 1987 and consecrated her life to the Lord Jesus Christ and to the preaching of the Gospel. In spite of great adversity, the Lord has been with her like a "mighty warrior" (Jeremiah 20:11).

Maria is active in the Catholic Charismatic Renewal of the Archdiocese of Miami. She has traveled around America, the Caribbean, Africa, and other nations bringing a message of faith, salvation and healing. She ministers the Word to prayer groups, as well as at the Miami Women's Detention Center and Genesis House, a home for the homeless with AIDS. She is a mother of four.

Library of Congress Number # 2002109722

Published by:
Queenship Publishing
P.O. Box 220
Goleta, CA 93116
(800) 647-9882 • (805) 692-0043 • Fax: (805) 967-5133

Printed in the United States of America

ISBN: 1-57918-199-6

ACKNOWLEDGMENTS

I dedicate this book in loving memory to
Fr. Harold F. Cohen, S.J.

A big thank you to:

My daughter Rosario for lending me her lap top.

The Beato family for their computer, love and kindness.

Fifi, Pat and Michael for their hospitality.

Ina and Mary for their encouragement, visions and dreams.

The King Jesus Prayer Group for their prayer support.

Mercedes for her faithfulness.

Rory, for her "computer help".

Kathy, for her help.

Ferro family for encouragement and support

Last, but not least, to the Precious Holy Spirit for guiding and inspiring me.

FORWARD

As you read this very practical spiritual book, *There's Power in Your Tongue*, I hope you will prayerfully ask the Lord to show you any areas of weakness that may exist in your life. My prayer for you is that the Holy Spirit will shine His powerful light though your heart, showing you any areas that should be dealt with, and even inspiring you to pray to rid yourself of any "leaven". Then you can start shoring up those weaknesses so you may be strong in the day of the Devil's attacks and able to resist the subtle compromises that he daily sends your way. Finally, it is my hope that reading *There's Power in Your Tongue* will help you to recapture any zeal for the Lord that you may have lost along the way.

Rev. Daniel F. Soyle, S.M.

INTRODUCTION

Proverbs 18:21 "Death and life are in the power of the tongue, and those who love it will eat its fruit."

Few verses in the Bible have impacted my life as much as this one. The moment I understood how powerful our words can be, I repented for the wrong use of my tongue and asked the Holy Spirit to take control of it.

We can use our tongues to bless or to curse, to encourage or discourage, to edify or tear down, to bring healing or destruction. With our tongues we grumble, complain, criticize, gossip, slander and pass judgment on others. Our words are packed with power for good or evil, and basically what we say is what we get; we "eat its fruits."

As Christians, we walk by faith and not by sight; faith in God's Word, in His promises. Therefore, we must align our words with what God says in the Bible. We must enter into agreement with our God. To possess the "promised life," to walk in victory over the devil, to bring glory to the Lord Jesus Christ, to extend God's kingdom, our tongues must be brought under control and into agreement with God's Word, which is His will. We are to become Christ-like, in His character and also in His power and authority, and our tongue must be submitted to the Holy Spirit in order to see good fruit.

I don't know what you're going through; I don't know the difficulties and the adversity that you are facing; but this much I know: The right or wrong use of your tongue will greatly influence how and when and if you will experience victory in that situation. Hosea 4:6 says "My people are destroyed for lack of knowledge." Don't let your tongue destroy you and those around you!

It's up to each one of us individually to ask the Holy Spirit to change our tongues from a deadly weapon into an instrument of blessing, because no "human being can tame the tongue, a restless evil, full of deadly poison." (James 3:8). As you submit your tongue to the Holy Spirit, you will start experiencing His transforming power. Our tongue is like a thermometer, our words reveal the state of our heart and the need to repent and change.

X

GRUMBLING AND COMPLAINING WILL GET YOU NOWHERE!

Proverbs 21:23: "He who keeps his mouth and his tongue keeps himself out of trouble."

The Israelites in the desert provide an excellent example of the negative effects of grumbling and complaining. They saw with their eyes the mighty signs and wonders, the awesome deliverance the Lord executed to bring them out of Egypt, the place of slavery; but only a few days into the desert they grumbled and complained because of unbelief when they faced the Red Sea before them and Pharaoh behind them. "What have you done to us, in bringing us out of Egypt…." (Exodus 14:10-12). They were gripped with fear and they quickly forgot the power of their Almighty God, for "whom nothing is impossible." (Luke 1:37). They also forgot that they were slaves in Egypt and had been crying out to God for deliverance. In Exodus 3:7-8, the Lord tells Moses "I have seen the affliction of my people who are in Egypt, and have heard their cry because of their taskmasters; I know their sufferings and I have come down to deliver them out of the hand of the Egyptians, and to bring them up out of that land to a good and broad land, a land flowing with milk and honey…" The Lord not only delivered them out of the hand of the enemy, but wanted to take them into a good land, the Promised Land, their inheritance, where they could be free and blessed as His people. In our lives the Lord delivers us out of the hand of the enemy, a hard taskmaster, a land of slavery to sin, and into the "promised life," a new life where we can experience freedom from slavery to sin and satan and we can experience the abundant life Jesus came to give. By the way, if you are blocked on all sides, like the Israelites were, with the Red Sea ahead of them and Pharaoh and his army behind them, and you don't know where to turn, don't grumble and complain, the Lord will make a way. He opened the Red Sea for the Israelites, didn't He? He will do the same for you, for the Lord "is the same yesterday, today, and forever." (Hebrews 13:8).

Romans 8:32 says that "He who did not spare his own Son but

gave him up for us all, will he not also give us all things with him?" Let's face it, our Heavenly Father has already given us the most important gift: His beloved Son, Jesus! Apart from Him, there is no life, no salvation, no redemption, no eternal life, no hope, no adoption into God's family. It cost Jesus His life, so that we could receive life! Imagine the Father's pain when Jesus became the sacrificial lamb on our behalf! And still we doubt the Father's provision for the rest of our needs! We're just like the Israelites!

Three days after the miracle of the parting of the Red Sea, where the Israelites crossed on dry ground and that same water destroyed their enemies, they grumbled and complained because of lack of water; it was as if their awesome God all of a sudden became powerless to work another miracle on their behalf. They not only murmured but wished for death. (Exodus 16:23). Eventually, God gave them what their tongues confessed.

It was God's perfect plan and will to take them to the Promised Land and to posses it; yet of those that left Egypt twenty years of age or older, not one of them entered the Promised Land except for Joshua and Caleb. They died in the desert as the result of their stubborn hearts filled with unbelief, which manifested in grumbling and complaining against Moses, and ultimately, the Lord. The Israelites in the desert had a pattern of murmuring, grumbling and complaining every time they faced any obstacle; by the time they got to the Promised Land they didn't have the faith to take it over. Psalm 78:22 says that "they had no faith in God and did not trust his saving power."

In Numbers 13, Moses sends twelve spies into the Promised Land, "the land of Canaan, which I (God) give to the people of Israel." The twelve spies were leaders of the Israelites, Joshua and Caleb included. The Lord had given them the land; now it was time to take a good look at it and bring back a report on this land. They spent forty days "spying" the land and came back with a "negative report;" the only two spies that were not in agreement with this report were Joshua and Caleb. The spies said, "We came to the land to which you sent us; it flows with milk and honey, and this is its fruit. YET, the people who dwell in the land are strong, and the cities are fortified and very large; and besides . . ." The ten negative spies just focused on the difficulties and forgot that their God was with them, and that He had promised them this land. Watch out when God gives you His Word, His promise, about something, and instead of believing Him you focus on the difficulties and you add a preposition YET or BUT to your response; "I know that the Lord still heals today, BUT the doctor said that the type of cancer I have is the worst kind!" If you have that kind of response, you're not believing, but rather focusing on the negative. Most probably you will not see God move powerfully in your life; because "without faith it is impossible to please God." (Hebrews 11:6).

Caleb, on the other hand, said, "Let us go up at once, and occupy it; for we are well able to overcome it." Caleb focused on God and His promise, knowing thãt what God had promised His people He would fulfill. The negative spies said "We are not able to go up against the people; for they are stronger than we are . . . . So they brought to the people of Israel an evil report of the land ...." The sad story is that the Israelites believed the evil report and refused to trust God. They grumbled, complained, wept, wished for death and even wanted to choose a captain to go back to Egypt! (Numbers 14). God finally got fed up with them and in verse 11 "The Lord said to Moses "How long will this people despise me? And how long will they not believe in me, in spite of all the signs which I have wrought among them?" When we despise the Word of God, we are despising Him. Proverbs 13:13 says "He who despises the Word brings destruction on himself..." When we refuse to believe, we will not see His glory and bring destruction upon ourselves because of disobedience. The ten spies that brought the evil, negative report died by plague, and the rest of the congregation had to wander in the desert; they went around in circles for the next forty years, until each one that had left Egypt twenty years or older had died in the desert, never entering the Promised Land, except for Joshua and Caleb, who believed God and His promise. A journey that would have taken eleven days turned into forty years! God judged them for their murmuring, grumbling and complaining, which resulted from their unbelief and their focus on their circumstances. It's our choice to believe God's report, the Bible, or the evil, negative report. To enter into the "promised life," to receive His promises and blessings, we have to believe God and take Him at His Word.

Where do you want to go with your life? Do you want to keep going in circles, never entering into the promise of God? TAKE CONTROL OF YOUR TONGUE! Do you want the Lord Jesus to be glorified in your life? Do you want to serve God effectively? TAKE CONTROL OF YOUR TONGUE! Do you want to experience God's blessings in every area of your life? START USING YOUR TONGUE FOR LIFE AND NOT FOR DEATH!

James 3:2-4 says that our tongue is like the bit in the horse's mouth and like the rudder in a ship; depending how we use it we will or will not make it to our destination. "If we put bits into the mouths of horses that they may obey us, we guide their whole bodies. Look at the ships also, though they are so great and are driven by strong winds, they are guided by a very small rudder wherever the will of the pilot directs." Just like the bit and the rudder, the tongue is a small member of our body but we must take control of it in order to get where we want to go. When we take control of our tongue, we are able to Control the body.

In 1 Corinthians 10:9-10, the Apostle Paul refers to the Israelites in the desert and writes "We must not put the Lord to the test, as some of them did and were destroyed by serpents; nor grumble, as some of them did and were destroyed by the Destroyer." Grumbling, complaining, murmuring and negativity is a sure way to attract evil spirits into our lives, and they come to "steal, kill and destroy" God's blessings and promises from us. (John 10:10). When we use our tongue for evil, what is manifested in our lives is death, not life. When we grumble, complain and confess negativity, we are really confessing what the devil wants us to say; we are confessing his "report;" and those are words that produce death, not life.

In 1992, when both our finances and marriage were destroyed, we had to put our beautiful home for sale. At that time the real estate market was "dead" in Miami, due to problems in the economy. Many came to me with a "negative report," saying that "your house will never sell at this time." There were beautiful homes for sale across the street from us that had been on the market for seven or eight months and they had not sold. I refused to believe the negative report, knowing that the Lord was with me and that somehow He would help me in this situation, for "No one who believes in Him will be put to shame." (Romans 10:11). I asked the Holy Spirit for guidance as to how to pray specifically for the house to be sold. The Holy Spirit had me cover the entire property with the Blood of Jesus, north, south, east and west; He instructed me to "march" around the house seven times, just like Joshua and the Israelites around Jericho; as I went around the house I was praising and thanking the Lord with a loud voice. I used also the gift of tongues and I broke any curse or any hold that satan had over the property in the Name of Jesus and by the Blood of Jesus. My house sold within two and one-half weeks! Everyone was surprised and amazed at the speed of the sale! Glory to God!

I hope by now you're convinced that grumbling and complaining will not get you out of your situation and into the destiny God has for you. We walk by faith, not by sight; we focus on the Lord and His promises, not on the difficulties. We have a choice either to believe or not believe God and to align our words with His. Let's speak life and not death in order to make it into our destiny. Don't use your tongue to spread a negative report, but rather to build up people's faith! The entire congregation of Israel believed the ten spies' negative report and never entered into their destiny. Are you tired of going around in circles, never getting anywhere?

Psalm 141:3 "Set a guard over my mouth, O Lord, keep watch over the door of my lips!"

CRITICISM IS THE ROAD TO DESTRUCTION

Psalm 34:12-13 "What man is there who desires life, and covets many days, that he may enjoy good? Keep your tongue from evil, and your lips from speaking deceit."

In Numbers 12, Miriam and Aaron complained and criticized Moses, the servant of God, of whom God had said there is none humbler (v.3). They complained and criticized him because of Moses' marriage to a Cushite; I believe the real reason was jealousy. Their jealousy was manifested in criticism, and the Lord heard those words! Ps. 105:15 says "Touch not my anointed ones, do my prophets no harm." It's messy when we "touch" God's anointed servants! The Lord told Miriam and Aaron (v.8) "Why then were you not afraid to speak against my servant Moses?" As a result of this "speaking" against Moses, Miriam became leprous, and ultimately she held back the entire Israelite nation from moving forward for a whole week.

The Pharisees, the most religious of all, had a critical spirit; they were proud and unteachable, and filled with jealousy; time after time we read as they approached Jesus with wrong motives, trying to "catch him." They were unwilling to change and ended up killing the King of Glory.

It's easy for us to become critical of one another, "experts" in people's weaknesses and defects, especially with the ones the Lord has placed over us. This not only displeases God, but all of this criticism and negativity will come back to us, for with "...the measure you give will be the measure you get back." (Luke6:38). (This verse applies to more than our finances!)

Could you have a case of spiritual leprosy in your life? Could it be that your wrong use of your tongue is holding back your healing, or holding back your family from possessing the promises of God?

Proverbs 11:9 "With his mouth the godless man would destroy his neighbor...." Get out of the road of criticism and into the road of intercession!

QUIT THE ROAD OF ACCUSATIONS!

Ps. 39:1 "I said, I will guard my ways, that I may not sin with my tongue, I will bridle my mouth...."

The ministry of accusation is the ministry of the devil. He's the accuser of the brethren (Revelation 12:10). When we point the finger and accuse others, we're carrying on with the work of the devil. When we have a problem with a brother or sister, how about going to them and speak "the truth in love?" (Ephesians 4:15). How about taking in to the Lord, rather than telling the whole church or group? In Isaiah 58 the Lord speaks about the kind of fast that pleases Him: it includes taking away the pointing of the finger and speaking wickedness.

There's supposed to be a healthy diversity in the Body of Christ. Even though we are all part of the body, we are not all alike. Each one of us has different gifts and functions, just as every organ in a human body has different functions, even though they're part of the same body. For example, don't point the finger at people when they worship in a different style or pray in a different way that you are not used to; it not only displeases the Lord, but you might have to face negative consequences as a result of the wrong use of your tongue. Again, Jesus says "....the measure you give will be the measure you get." (Matt.7:2). The apostle Paul says in Galatians 6:7 "...for whatever a man sows, that he will also reap." What you say about others is what's coming back to you!

We must learn to discern what is happening to us. Why am I saying these things? Why am I so upset? Is there a wrong spirit in me? If not, you might find yourself being used by the enemy to create disunity and conflict in His Body. Remember the power of your words! The enemy knows that a house divided cannot stand. An easy way to destroy a person's reputation or a prayer group is to use our tongues for evil; we really don't need a knife or a gun!

Don't point the finger and accuse God's delegated authority over your life. In Numbers 16, Korah, Dathan, and Abiram rebelled against Aaron and Moses in the desert and accused them of pride and of lording their power and authority over the Israelites.

They told Moses and Aaron "…why then do you exalt yourselves above the assembly of the Lord?" They created dissension and disunity and took with them "250 leaders of the congregation, chosen from the assembly, well-known men; and they assembled themselves together against Moses and Aaron." The Lord didn't like it one bit, because Moses and Aaron were His delegated authority over His people; the Lord himself brought judgment upon those men! They were stubborn and unrepentant and finally we see that "the ground under them split asunder; and the earth opened its mouth and swallowed them up, with their households….." That's right, that's what their tongues brought them: death itself! Acts 23:5 says "….for it is written, You shall not speak evil of a ruler of your people."

Jesus Himself was wrongly accused time and time again. He was accused of being a "glutton and a drunkard" (Matt.11:19); of having a demon (John 7:20); of being a Samaritan (John 8:48); of being a "perverter of the nation" (Luke 23:2); of being a "blasphemer" (Matt. 26:65); of being an "impostor" (Matt. 27:63); and an "evildoer" (John 18:30). None of these accusations could be further from the truth! The devil used Jesus' enemies to carry on with his ministry of lies and accusations against Him; they definitely used their tongues for death, not life, and death is what they got; Jesus told the Pharisees in John 8:24 "I told you that you would die in your sins, for you will die in your sins unless you believe that I am he."

Proverbs 12:13 "An evil man is ensnared by the transgression of his lips…"

FLATTERY IS NOT THE WAY

Proverbs 12:3-4 "May the Lord cut off all flattering lips, the tongue that makes great boasts, those who say "With our tongue we will prevail, our lips are with us; who is our master?"

Flattery is trying to control and manipulate; it is a form of deceit and hypocrisy. Dishonest people use flattery to gain advantage over others (Jude 16). Your heart is not conformed to the Word of God and you're trying to get your own way rather than trusting in the Lord. You have a hidden agenda. Psalm 78:36-37 says about the Israelites in the desert that "they flattered Him with their mouths; they lied to Him with their tongues. Their heart was not steadfast toward Him; they were not true to His covenant."

Absalom, King David's son, used flattery to steal "the hearts of the men of Israel" in order to steal the throne from his father (2 Samuel 15:6). He had a hidden agenda and got what he wanted for a little while, until God reversed the situation. His life ended tragically (2 Samuel 18:15). Self-promotion through flattery does not work in the Kingdom. Psalm 75:6-7 says "For not from the east or from the west and not from the wilderness comes lifting up; but it is God who executes judgment, putting down one and lifting up another."

In the world, flattery is a common way of getting on somebody's "good side." This does not work with God; He knows your heart; you can fool other people, but you can't fool God, even when you use the "right words" or the "right prayers." Matthew quotes from the prophet Isaiah (Matt. 15:8): "This people honors me with their lips, but their heart is far from me…" I see so many people coming before God with the "right words" and the "right prayers;" they come to prayer group and when they don't receive what they want when they want it, they drop out and start looking for results somewhere else apart from God. Sometimes when they receive what they want you never see them again! The Lord delights in blessing us; He's our heavenly Father and wants to meet all our needs; still, He's more interested in our hearts and in relationship. Jesus said in John 17:3 "And this is eternal life, that they know thee the only true God, and Jesus Christ whom thou has sent." The Lord wants intimacy with us; He wants to be close to us! He wants us to experience His love! We don't need to pretend before God; as a matter of fact, what pleases Him is "a broken and contrite heart." (Psalm 51:17).

The prophet Ezekiel says about "church" people in chapter 33:31: "And they come to you as people come, and they sit before you as my people, and they hear what you say but they will not do it; for with their lips they show much love, but their heart is set on their gain." Do you know "church" people that never change their ways, even though they attend church?

Let's look at some "flattery" verses and their negative consequences:

Proverbs 26:28 "A lying tongue hates its victims, and a flattering mouth works ruin."

Proverbs 29:5 "A man who flatters his neighbor spreads a net for his feet."

Daniel 11:32 says about the enemy that "He shall seduce with flattery those who violate the covenant;...." Flattery is a weapon the enemy uses to seduce us by tickling our ears. Don't we love to be complimented!

Romans 16:17-18: The apostle Paul tells us to avoid people that through their "flattering words they deceive the hearts of the simple-minded."

There's no room for flattery in God's kingdom. It simply will not work.......and it's harmful! It will get you in trouble.

YOUR WORDS CAN GET YOU OFF TRACK!

Matthew 12:36 "I tell you, on the day of judgment men will render account for every careless word they utter; for by your words you will be justified, and by your words you will be condemned."

If these words of Jesus do not shake you up, if they don't motivate you to change your ways and the wrong use of your tongue, I don't know what will! He's not talking here about a rapist, a serial killer or a robber. He's referring to the use of our words; all those stupid, nasty, derogatory, negative comments and gossip. And we thought they were so harmless!

The Lord Jesus had more to say about our words. Matthew 5:20 happens to be one of the hardest parts in the Bible. Jesus said: "But I say to you that every one who is angry with his brother shall be liable to judgment; whoever insults his brother shall be liable to the council, and whoever says you fool, shall be liable to the hell of fire." Nice words! Who has not used their tongue in this fashion? And judgment and hell are our just deserts! Once again we see that our words have consequences of life and death. We usually "minimize" the effects of our wrong use of words, but words can wound us deeply. In Psalm 52:2, David speaks of the tongue of his enemy as being "like a sharp razor;" in other words, they pierce right where it hurts! In Psalm 64:2-3, again David refers to the tongue of the wicked as "swords" and their "bitter words like arrows." They are meant to destroy and hurt! People's reputations can be destroyed by the sins of our mouth; gossip, slander, criticism, for example, can easily destroy a prayer group and even a church! James says that "the tongue is a fire. The tongue is an unrighteous world among our members, staining the whole body, setting on fire the cycle of nature, and set on fire by hell." (James 3:6).

We've seen how the enemy used the ministry of accusation against Jesus during His public ministry. However, during His passion I believe that the wrong use of the tongue was one of His greatest sufferings. Human tongues were used to lie about Him, to accuse Him, to deride Him, to mock Him, to insult Him, to scoff Him, to ridicule Him, to provoke Him. Words may not have nailed Him physically to the Cross, but they pierced His Sacred Heart!

Many of the sins the Apostle Paul mentions in Ephesians 4 and 5 have to do with the wrong use of our tongues. Let's look at some of the passages:

Ephesians 4:29 "Let no evil talk come out of your mouths…"

Ephesians 4:31 "Let all bitterness and wrath and anger and clamor and slander be put away from you…"

Ephesians 5:4 "Let there be no filthiness, nor silly talk, nor levity…"

Ephesians 5:6 "Let no one deceive you with empty words, for it is because of these things that the wrath of God comes upon the sons of disobedience."

In the Book of Colossians the Apostle Paul had similar things to say:

Colossians 3:8 "But now put them all away; anger, wrath, malice, slander, and foul talk from your mouth."

Colossians 3:9 "Do not lie to one another…"

So much of the world's ways have entered the Church, that most of us act and talk exactly as the people in the world. "Dirty jokes" are as common as apple pie! We swear and say things that we don't really mean; we make promises we can't keep and think this is normal! It used to be that a man's word was as good as a legal contract; not anymore! We lie and call it "white lies;" but lying, any kind of lying is not of God, but of the devil, who is a "liar and father of all lies." (John 8:44). Jesus says in Matthew 5:37 "…let your yes be yes and your no be no. For whatever is more than these is from the evil one." (NKJ). Look at what James says: "But above all, my brethren, do not swear, either by heaven or by earth or with any other oath, but let your yes be yes and your no be no, that you may not fall under condemnation." Condemnation is what we deserve when we don't speak truthfully! God' ways are simply different than ours!

Let's take a look at some proverbs regarding the wrong use of our tongue and the negative consequences they bring about:

Proverbs 16:28 "A perverse man spreads strife, and a whisperer separates close friends."

Proverbs 17:20 "A man of crooked mind does not prosper, and one with a perverse tongue falls into calamity." (We have seen how the tongues of the Israelites in the desert kept them from God's destiny and finally got what they asked for: death!)

Proverbs 18:6-7 "A fool's lips bring strife, and his mouth invites a flogging. A fool's mouth is his ruin, and his lips are a snare to himself."

Proverbs 19:5 "A false witness will not go unpunished, and he who utters lies will not escape."

Proverbs 22:10 "Drive out a scoffer, and strife will go out, and quarreling and abuse will cease." Remember what happened to Korah and company?

Proverbs 30:32-33 "If you have been foolish, exalting yourself, or if you have been devising evil, put your hand on your mouth. For pressing milk produces curds, pressing the nose produces blood and pressing anger produces strife."

Proverbs 6:12-15 "A worthless person, a wicked man, goes about with crooked speech, winks with his eyes, scrapes with his feet, points with his finger, with perverted heart devises evil, continually sowing discord; therefore calamity will come upon him suddenly, in a moment he will be broken beyond healing."

OUR WORDS CAN TURN INTO CURSES!

Proverbs 26:2 "Like a sparrow in its flitting, like a swallow in its flying, a curse that is causeless does not alight."

When there's a curse in our lives and in our family tree, there's a reason for it; sin caused it. Many of the curses in our lives have come through the words that we say about ourselves or the words that others have pronounced over our lives. Remember, our words are packed with power; for good or for evil. Proverbs 6:2 says that you "are snared in the utterance of your lips, caught in the words of your mouth." Our words can snare or trap us and form a barrier that prevents God's blessings from entering into our lives.

For over six years I have been ministering at the women's jail. Most of these women have heard negative words spoken over their lives since they were small; words like "you'll never amount to anything;" "you are a hopeless case;" "you'll end up in jail;" "you are just like your Aunt Betty, stupid and dumb;" "you'll never change; you're a disaster." Because our words are packed with power and they have the power for "life or death," what has been negatively "prophesied" over people's lives actually comes to pass. Even psychologists have coined the term "the self-fulfilling prophecy!" Tell a child the same thing again and again and again and you will see it lived out in his life. It's difficult for a child, for example, to prosper in school when he's been told time and time again that he's stupid. He might even have a good I.Q., but he's not able to perform; he believes he's stupid.

In the book of Genesis 31, Jacob finally decides to leave his father-in-law (and uncle) Laban, and return home. In the meantime, his second wife, Rachel, who was his favorite wife, stole her father's household gods. No one knew. When Laban catches up with Jacob and company, Laban asks him "....but why did you steal my gods?" Jacob answers him that "Any one with whom you find your gods shall not live." Now Jacob did not know that Rachel had stolen them. Jacob cursed with his words whoever it was that stole Laban's gods, not knowing it was Rachel. In Genesis 35, we read that Rachel dies during labor. Jacob himself pronounced a curse over his favorite wife and it was fulfilled. He literally cursed her to death.

We can self-inflict a curse over ourselves by the things we say about ourselves: "I'm so stupid;" "I always mess up;" "I hate my body;" "I wish I was dead;" "I'm going crazy;" "this headache is killing me;" "I'll never be healed;" "I'll never find a good spouse;" on and on and on. Remember the Israelites in the desert that did not believe God and His Word, but instead believed the "negative report?" Well, as they confessed with their mouths their unbelief and negativity and wished for death, they never entered the Promised Land, but died in the desert. They cursed themselves!

Another way we can curse ourselves is by cursing our parents. Watch what you tell them and what you say about them! Proverbs 20:20 says "If one curses his father or his mother, his lamp will be put out in utter darkness." Darkness, blindness and confusion may come upon us if we have cursed our parents. The only commandment with promises attached to it is the one about honoring our parents. Deuteronomy 5:16 says "Honor your father and your mother, as the Lord your God commanded you; that your days may be prolonged, and that it may go well with you." I would even include here our spiritual fathers and mothers! I once ministered at a women's drug addiction home; as I was praying the Lord revealed to me that the root cause for these women's misery was their relationship with their parents. The Holy Spirit was right on target! Everyone needed healing, forgiveness and restoration with their parents. When I asked, "How many of you need to repent for how you've treated your parents, and how many of you need to forgive your parents?" Every single woman got up to repent and forgive and to talk to God! They were weeping profoundly and a great healing took place. Thank you, Jesus!

By now you might be thinking that it's really impossible for your tongue to change. And you're right! Apart from His grace you can't change! You cannot change by trying hard enough or by reading a self-help book. There is one person that can change you and His name is Jesus of Nazareth! Through the power of His Holy Spirit you can be transformed and empowered to live a new life, right here in this planet. Praise the Lord!

CHECK YOUR HEART!

Proverbs 4:23 "Keep your heart with all vigilance; for from it flow the springs of life."

There is a connection between your heart and your mouth. Jesus says in Matthew 12:34 that "out of the abundance of the heart the mouth speaks." In other words, what you have in your heart will affect your speech. Again in Matt. 15:18-19, Jesus says: "But those things which proceed out of the mouth come from the heart and they defile a man. For out of the heart proceed evil thoughts, murders, adulteries, fornications, thefts, false witness, blasphemies." In other words, defilement comes from inside; sin originates in the heart. The state of your heart and your faith level is revealed when you speak.

What have you stored in your heart? Unbelief, anger, unforgiveness, pride, greed, resentment, bitterness, sin, love of money, love of the world? It will show in your negative words! It's possible to go to Mass regularly and your life never change; it's possible to participate in religious activities and never change. Remember, the Holy Spirit wants to transform us into the image of Jesus Christ. This also includes using our tongues to bring life and not death. We don't want to be like the Pharisees, whom Jesus condemned. He called them hypocrites! In Mark 7:6, He says: "Well did Isaiah prophesy of you hypocrites, as it is written, this people honor me with their lips, but their heart is far from me..."

Sin originates in the heart, which in turn affects the words that you use, which in turn causes destruction or life in your life and the life of others. The prophet Jeremiah says the "the heart is deceitful above all things and desperately corrupt..." (Jeremiah 17:9). Romans 3:10-14 says "None is righteous, no, not even one; no one understands, no one seeks for God. All have turned aside, together they have gone wrong; no one does good, not even one. Their throat is an open grave, they use their tongues to deceive. The venom of asps is under their lips." This is the human condition.

Our words affect us and others. We saw how because the Israelites believed the negative report, they grumbled and complained and could not respond in faith to possess the land, and they never entered into their destiny; Joshua and Caleb, who believed, still had to walk in the desert for forty years as a consequence of others' unbelief. Because of Miriam's mouth she got leprosy and the entire Israelite nation was held back seven days without moving forward. Jacob cursed whoever stole Laban's idols, not knowing it was his wife Rachel, and she died prematurely. How about Korah, Dathan, and Abiram? Not only did they perish, but also their entire households were swallowed up because of their rebellion!

If you spend more time watching T.V. and reading secular material than reading the Word of God and praying, then the world has evangelized you and not the Lord Jesus. What you are storing in your heart are worldly ways of thinking and acting and they go against the Lord and His Word. You will not be able to move in faith when a difficulty arises and will probably believe the "negative report." For example, it's very difficult for people who don't know the Word of God, to believe God for their healing when they are sick; I know so because I've prayed with many of them! It's very difficult for people without faith to believe that the Lord loves them and knows them by name. In a moment of crisis they'll settle for the "negative report," just like the Israelites in the desert. Remember, "without faith it is impossible to please God." (Hebrews 11:6). And "whatever does not proceed from faith is sin." (Romans 14:22).

I remember the day my son Ricky broke a huge window trying to catch a lizard after I had told him to stop it. He broke the window and never caught the lizard; but what came out of my mouth were not nice words, but words packed with anger. Thank God for the Holy Spirit, who convicted me of the state of my heart! In James 3, he says about our tongue: "With it we bless the Lord and Father, and with it we curse men, who are made in the likeness of God. From the same mouth come blessing and cursing. My brethren, this ought not to be so." Isn't this what happens to many of us in the midst of heavy traffic?

Difficulties, trials and obstacles seem to squeeze out of our hearts what is really inside; they reveal stuff that we don't like. We say nasty things and later say we didn't really mean it, when in fact that is exactly what we meant when we "lost it."

What can we do about the state of our heart, which the Bible says is "desperately wicked?" How can we take control of our tongues?

JESUS IS THE WAY!

John 14:6 "I am the way, and the truth, and the life; no one comes to the Father, but by me."

Did you know that even for salvation we have to use our tongues, to proclaim Jesus as Lord and Savior of our lives? This is really using our tongues for LIFE! The apostle Paul says in Romans 10:9-10 that "...if you confess with your lips that Jesus is Lord and believe in your heart that God raised him from the dead, you will be saved. For man believes with his heart and so is justified, and he confesses with his lips and so is saved." In other words, once we believe with our hearts the message of the gospel, that fact that we are lost and bound for hell apart from Jesus Christ; once we believe that we need to repent and be forgiven and cleansed with the blood of Jesus to be accepted by the Father and to make it into heaven, a "confession" of faith has to be proclaimed with our mouths. This is very important because most of us have been baptized as babes and confirmed because our parents decided to (and praise God for that!); now as adults we need to take a stand and proclaim Jesus as Lord and Savior, from the heart, because we now believe it ourselves. When we do so, our lives will change because we have opened our hearts to the Lord Jesus and invited Him to be Lord and take control of our lives. This is the first and most important step; Jesus said "I am the door..." (John 10:9). Through Him we enter God's kingdom; through Him we are adopted into God's family. It's God's grace (undeserved gift) that saves us (Ephesians 2:8-9) and His grace enables us and empowers us, and now "I can do all things in him who strengthens me." (Phillipians 4:13). From now on my trust and my reliance for everything, including my tongue, is placed in the God of the universe, Jesus Christ, who "came to seek and to save the lost." (Luke 19:10).

If you have never invited Jesus into your life as Lord and Savior, and now you would like to do so, here's a prayer that needs to be "confessed with your lips," as the Apostle Paul states in Romans 10.

"Heavenly Father, I come before you this day as a repentant

sinner. Lord Jesus Christ, please forgive me of all my sins; cleanse me and wash me with your precious blood and make me white as snow. I open my heart to you, Lord Jesus, and invite you to come in as my personal Lord and Savior. I believe that on the Cross of Calvary you paid the penalty for all my sins and right now I transfer my trust for my salvation on your finished work at the Cross. I renounce sin, satan and all his lies. I only want to do your will from now on. Thank you, Jesus, for your gift of salvation and eternal life." Amen!

This is the most important step you can take in this life! Now you are ready to begin a new life with the Lord Jesus in the center of your heart and are heaven-bound, thanks to His mercy and grace. Because Jesus is now with you, you have power to overcome sin and satan as you rely on the Holy Spirit. Because the Lord Jesus is now with you, He'll help you to walk through every trial and difficulty; you are not alone! The grip of sin has been broken over your life; now the Lord Jesus is your Master, not sin. Now you have a "saved" tongue! If you need to forgive anyone who has harmed you, now is the time to do so. Forgiveness is a decision of your will, not an emotion; it's not an option but a command from the Lord.

As Catholics, we are blessed to have the Sacrament of Reconciliation! The last words the priest usually says is "Go in peace; your sins have been forgiven;" many need to hear these words many times until they truly believe from their hearts. These are life-giving words!

Dear reader, I encourage you to make frequent use of this Sacrament, so that you truly believe that "There is therefore now no condemnation for those who are in Christ Jesus"! (Romans 8.1)

GET FILLED WITH
THE OIL OF THE HOLY SPIRIT!

Now that Jesus is in our hearts, what is the next step to be taken in our new life in order to grow and become strong in the Lord?

Many of us are exactly like the Christians that the Apostle Paul encountered in Ephesus (Acts 19:1-2). Paul asked them if they had received the Holy Spirit, and they answered "No, we have never even heard that there is a Holy Spirit." Many of us have received the Holy Spirit in Baptism and Confirmation, but in reality we live without His power in our lives. His presence in our lives is not noticeable to us or to those around us. We look like everybody else; there's no difference between us and Joe Pagan. The Holy Spirit is grieved and imprisoned inside of us and we need to let Him out. Let's take a look at what the Apostle Paul says to do:

Ephesians 5:18-21 "And do not get drunk with wine, for that is debauchery; but be filled with the Spirit, addressing one another in psalms and hymns and spiritual songs, singing and making melody to the Lord with all your heart, always and for everything giving thanks in the name of our Lord Jesus Christ to God the Father. Be subject to one another."

The first thing that I want to say is that getting filled with the Holy Spirit is not a one time thing; in the Greek it means to be continuously getting filled! This means everyday, or many times a day, as you need. When we get filled with the Holy Spirit (or baptized in the Holy Spirit), our lives will change because our hearts have changed; our tongues will also experience a change. We receive a new vocabulary. Remember that there's a connection between our hearts and our tongues; a clean and pure heart will produce a different vocabulary than a filthy heart. This is the result of the Holy Spirit working is us, as we yield to Him, not the result of "trying hard." The first thing that happens to us is that our vocabulary will change and we will speak to one another in a different way. Instead of "evil talk" (Ephesians 4:29), what will come out of our mouths will be "only such as is good for edifying....that it may impart grace to those who hear." Our words will be packed with hope and encouragement, because with the Lord Jesus there is always hope! His mercies are "new every morning; great is His faithfulness!" (Lamentations 3:23). It's not by accident that usually the first gift manifested after the release of the Holy Spirit in a person's life is the gift of tongues. Our tongues need to be "sanctified," and when we speak in tongues we are speaking with the right words according to God's perfect will. It's the Holy Spirit inside of us together with our spirit praying the perfect prayer or praising God, without offending anyone. Although we don't know exactly what we're saying, we know that we are proclaiming life with our tongues, because the Holy Spirit is the Lord and Giver of Life. This is one gift that helps us to grow in holiness; "He who speaks in a tongue edifies himself..." (1 Corinthians 14:4). Recently, I was in California speaking and ministering to a group of ladies; I used the gift of tongues, and afterwards an older lady came up to me and told me that I had been speaking in Aramaic, and I was saying "Holy Spirit, Holy Spirit, comfort me." Isn't that powerful? The Holy Spirit is indeed our comforter, not drugs and alcohol! In Acts 2:4, the followers of Jesus, including Mother Mary, "were all filled with the Holy Spirit and began to speak in other tongues, as the Spirit gave them utterance."

The second change that takes place is that we will have a new song in our hearts and we will be singing to our Lord "with all your heart." (Ps. 40:3). You will become joyful and this will spill out of your heart, touching everyone around you. The Holy Spirit is the spirit of joy; joy is a fruit of the Holy Spirit (Galatians 5). Joy is not the absence of troubles and adversity, but rather having the Lord present in your heart. Jesus was filled with the "oil of gladness" (Hebrews 1:9b); He had an anointing of joy over His life that kept Him strong in facing adversity. He wants to do the same for us! In Isaiah 61, the Lord says that He wants to give those who mourn "a garland instead of ashes, the oil of gladness instead of mourning, the mantle of praise instead of a faint spirit." When you are filled with the joy of the Lord, depression leaves and laughter is what comes out of your mouth; laughter and kind words; not words of grumbling, complaining, criticism, anger, gossip. Recently in Trinidad, I was leading a retreat, and the Holy Spirit came upon a group of people around me and they started to laugh uncontrollably; the lady next to me was bending over as she laughed! She couldn't stand straight! It turned out that this lady's husband had recently passed away and she had been very depressed....until that moment! The Holy Spirit Himself ministered to her by filling her with His joy, for the "joy of the Lord is your strength." (Nehemiah 8:10). The Holy Spirit will minister to us whatever we need at every step of the way. In today's world we especially need the joy of the Lord to remain strong and not depressed. People in the world are joyless; they need alcohol and drugs to make it. But as God's people, we have His Holy Spirit, who fills us with joy. Psalm 16:11 says "...in thy presence there is fullness of joy". It's our choice to remain depressed or to enter into His presence daily, and receive the fullness of joy that abounds in Him!

The third change in our hearts will be that we will be thanking God in every situation (unlike the Israelites!). You will experience an attitude change. Instead of grumbling and complaining in difficult situations, or blaming others, you will instead thank the Lord, "for this is the will of God in Christ Jesus for you. Do not quench the Spirit." (1Thessalonians 5:18-19). Like the prophet Jonah, let's cry out to our God "with the voice of thanksgiving" in the midst of our troubles. (Jonah 2:9). My nephew Bill, 29 years old, went to the bank to get a loan to open his own business. One banker told him that only a miracle would enable him to receive that loan. My nephew answered that "if all I need is a miracle, my Father specializes in that." Instead of grumbling and complaining, he released his faith and started to thank the Lord in advance. He got his loan! Alleluia! Having an attitude of gratitude and thanking the Lord moves His powerful right arm. As we thank the Lord from the heart and we release our faith in Him and in His Word, the Holy Spirit is released to move on our behalf. Faith attracts the Holy Spirit. This is evident in the ministry of Jesus. The feeding of the 5,000, the feeding of the 4,000 and the resurrection of Lazarus were preceded by thanksgiving. To enter the presence of God is preceded by thanksgiving, not by grumbling, complaining and whining. "Enter his gates with thanksgiving; His courts with praise." (Ps.100:4). We stay outside the "gates" if we try to come in with grumbling and complaining. In the same way that praise and thanks-giving attract the Holy Spirit, nasty, negative talk grieves the Holy Spirit and attracts demonic power! (See Numbers 21: 5-6).

If you constantly speak words of death, like "I hate my husband," you may be inviting a spirit of hatred and anger into your life and home; if fear is expressed in your talk, for example, "I fear tomorrow," you may be inviting a spirit of fear to keep you tormented and afraid. If you and your husband or your children are constantly arguing and bickering, you may be inviting a spirit of strife to enter your home and create division and disunity. Watch your tongue! Praise God for the Holy Spirit, "for God did not give us a spirit of timidity (or fear), but a spirit of power and love and self-control." (2 Timothy 1:7). Watch out for those careless words! On the day of judgment we will have to render account for them! (Matthew 12:36). Isn't it time for us to stop, and honestly take an inventory of the use of our tongue? Aren't these words of Jesus enough to have us cry out to the Lord in repentance, asking the Holy Spirit to take control of our tongues?

During a time of great adversity in my life, when we had lost everything, Ricky's school called and said that he needed a haircut by the next day, or else he would not be allowed in school. I did not have money for a haircut, and I did not know where my separated husband was. I talked to the Lord about my situation, laid everything in His hands and started to confess my trust in Him and that I knew He would provide. I thanked Him and reminded Him that Ricky was His son and therefore Ricky's need would be met. I left the house and went to minister at a home with the homeless with AIDS. Suddenly, a friend of mine showed up unexpectedly and handed me $50 the Holy Spirit had asked her to give me. She said that she "knew she would find me there," and there I was. Thank God I didn't stay home having a pity party and feeling sorry for myself!

Going back to the Israelites in the desert, it is evident that as they grumbled and complained and wished for death, the Holy Spirit was grieved, and what was activated were the evil spirits. An atmosphere of negativity, depression, fear, grumbling, attracts the enemy. That is the kind of atmosphere he feels at home in. The opposite is true: an atmosphere of thanksgiving, faith and praise, where the name of Jesus is being lifted up and glorified, will expel the enemy from our lives and we will experience His presence, power, freedom, healing, peace, deliverance and victory in our lives. Ps. 22:3 says that the Lord is "enthroned on the praises of Israel (His people)." When King Jesus shows up, great things happen; we are changed and transformed! In our ladies prayer group, we've seen a number of instantaneous healings as we thanked and praised God. One lady's elbow was "suddenly" healed as she was thanking and praising the Lord. She had walked into the prayer meeting with a broken elbow; it was awesome to see her moving and bending her elbow! Thank you, Jesus!

The fourth thing that will happen in your heart is that you will be "subject to one another out of reverence for Christ." Paul says in Philippians 2:3 to "count others better than yourselves." If the Church (us) moved in this kind of humility, the world by now would know that we are truly the Body of Christ; that our God is real. The world teaches us that we are #1 and to look out for #1; the Word teaches us that the Lord is #1 and to love our neighbors as ourselves. Submission means glorifying the Lord Jesus in every situation and in our relationships; it means to submit ourselves to the authority over us. This includes, of course, control of our tongues. I hope by now the Holy Spirit Himself has convinced you of your need for Him!

FILL UP WITH THE WORD OF GOD!

> Colossians 3:16 "Let the word of Christ dwell in you richly, as you teach and admonish one another in all wisdom, and as you sing psalms and hymns and spiritual songs with thankfulness in your hearts to God."

Notice the similar effects that both the Holy Spirit and the Word of God produce in our hearts: a new vocabulary; a new song and joy; humility, as we submit to one another and treat one another differently; and gratitude in our hearts. They are both necessary.

It was only after the Holy Spirit was released in my life that I had a desire for the Word of God; not only did I have this desire, but I could actually understand the Bible for the first time in my life! This is something the Holy Spirit imparts to a believer: a hunger for the Word of God and the understanding of the Word; after all, He is the author of the Bible! Jesus said: "Man shall not live by bread alone, but by every word that proceeds from the mouth of God." This means that you are to feed on this Word many times a day, like newborn babes craving for milk (1 Peter 2:2). How many times a day do you eat food? At least three times a day! We know that we need food to stay alive and healthy; it's the same for our spiritual growth! We need to "eat" the Word of God in order to grow up, have our minds renewed and become strong. The prophet Jeremiah says in chapter 15:16 "Thy words were found, and I ate them, and thy words became to me a joy and the delight of my heart…." The Lord told the prophet Ezequiel in chapter 3:3 to "eat this scroll that I give you and FILL YOUR STOMACH with it. Then I ate it; and it was in my mouth as sweet as honey." We are to fill up with the Word of God, not just a nibble here and a nibble there.

As I preach and teach and minister to different groups of Catholics in America and other parts of the world, I find that most of them have tremendous lack of appetite for the Word; they are anemic and have settled for the junk food the world offers and have no hunger for the real thing, which is the Word of God.

The Word of God in our hearts produces faith; faith comes by hearing and hearing the Word of God (Romans 10:17) (NKJ).

If our hearts are filled with the Word of God, which are words of life, we will proclaim words that bring life and not death. Remember there is a connection between the heart and the words that we speak. In Mass, we make positive confessions of faith with our tongues a number of times; that's excellent, because we are proclaiming words of life! Expect healings in your life when you receive the Eucharist, after all, we tell the Lord "…but just say the Word and I shall be healed." When we proclaim the responsorial Psalm together, we are proclaiming and confessing the Word of God over our lives; expect and trust the Lord to move on your behalf! He says that "I am watching over my word to perform it." (Jeremiah 1:12). So many times I've gone to Mass with a need, and it so happens that what I needed to confess and proclaim is exactly the Psalm or the Gospel for that day; as I have believed and confessed and trusted in the Lord and His Word, I've seen His provision in my life, especially with my finances.

Consider the attitude of Mother Mary; she "treasured" everything about her Son, the Word, in her heart. Why is this important? Because our believing is in the heart, not the mind; faith is in the heart, and "faith comes by hearing and hearing the Word of God" (Romans 10:17) (NKJ) and "without faith it is impossible to please God" (Hebrews 11:16). As God's people we walk by faith, not by sight! We walk by revelation! True Biblical faith, the kind that pleases God, is based on His Word! And we can certainly believe God and His Word, His promises, because "God is not man, that he should lie, or a son of man, that he should repent. Has he said, and will he not do it? Or has he spoken, and will he not fulfill it?" (Numbers 23:19). There's a promise of provision for every need and lack that we experience in this planet. The Word of God says in 2 Corinthians 1:20 that all the promises of God are "yes" and "amen" in Christ Jesus! This means that as Jesus is seated at the right hand of the Father interceding on our behalf, He sits there as the Word, as the Promise, and every time the Father looks at His beloved Son, the Father is reminded of His Word and His promises, and He cannot go against the Word! God simply cannot go against His Word; if He says it, that settles it! I believe it! Don't settle for the negative report, settle for His report! Stand on His Word! Confess it with your mouth! But to have this kind of faith, you must get into the Word yourself, and allow the Word to enter your heart! Only then will you become strong and grow up. It's your choice to remain in Pampers all your life, sucking your thumb in the pew of the Church, or choose to grow up and become the godly person that God created you to be. It's time for all God's people to rise up and join His army!

When the Holy Spirit makes the Word of God alive, it becomes the strongest force in the universe. Think of how the world was created. Let's look at Genesis 1:2: "The earth was without form and void, and darkness was upon the face of the deep; and the Spirit of God was moving over the face of the waters." Verse 3 says "And God said . . . ." When God said it, it was done! Ps. 147:15 says "He sent out His command to the earth; His word runs very swiftly." The Lord told the Prophet Jeremiah in chapter 1:12 ". . .For I am watching over my word to perform it." Perform what? His commands, so that His purposes are accomplished. Ps. 33:6 "By the word of the Lord the heavens were made, and all their host by the breath of his mouth." Ps. 107:20 says that "He sent forth His word, and healed them, and delivered them from destruction." Isaiah 55:11 "so shall my word be that goes forth from my mouth; it shall not return to me empty, but it shall accomplish that which I purpose, and prosper in the thing for which I sent it." In the Book of Ezekiel 37, the valley of dry bones rose up to become an "exceedingly great army" through the Spirit and the Word. My dear brothers and sisters, God does not move apart from the Word. He has given us the Bible so that we can come to know Him more and more and more... It bothers me to see so many church-going Catholics so ignorant of the Word of God! St. Jerome, one of the early Fathers of the Church, said that "ignorance of Scripture is ignorance of Christ."

Apart from Jesus Christ, the Word made flesh, our lives are void, without meaning and purpose, and in darkness. When the Holy Spirit comes upon us, the spirit of revelation, He makes Jesus and His Word real and alive in our hearts. When your tongue is surrendered to the Holy Spirit and your heart is filled with the Word, you truly will be transformed into an instrument of blessing! With a surrendered tongue to the Lord, you will start speaking words of life and not death. The Israelites in the desert voiced their desire for death so frequently, that they received what they confessed; they died and never entered into their destiny. We must use our tongues in agreement with God's Word to get to where we want to go and to receive all that God has for us. We must become doers of the Word (James 1:22), and not just listeners.

In 1992 my life as I knew it collapsed. My marriage broke and we lost our finances, both at the same time; but by God's grace I did not collapse, but rather experienced the sustaining power that comes from the Word of God. The Holy Spirit had been previously released in my life in 1987, and for years I fed on the Word with great hunger; I came to know and believe the promises of God in the Scriptures. When the "bad times" came, I knew my God and knew that to stand on His Word was to stand on solid rock, not on sinking sand. I knew in Whom I believed. That's what kept me standing! That's what kept me encouraged and not discouraged! That's what kept me joyful and not depressed! It was difficult not to focus on the circumstances and keep my focus on the Lord Jesus, but with the help of our precious Holy Spirit, we can "do all things in Him who strengthens me" (Phillipians 4:13). Most nights I had to claim God's Word in Ps.127:2, which says that the Lord "gives to His beloved sleep." I knew I would not be able to sleep on my own, because the circumstances were so negative, so I proceeded to proclaim and claim His promises, and every night I slept like a baby! Thank you, Jesus!

The enemy, that "liar and father of lies" (John 8:44), proceeded to torment me with many negative thoughts about my children; thoughts like "they'll never amount to anything;" "your children will never make it;" "your children will never be healed or be able to recover from the trauma of a broken home;" on, and on, and on, until I learned to rebuke that liar with the truth of God's Word, the Sword of the Spirit. I used Ps. 37:25, which says "I have been young, and now am old; yet I have not seen the righteous forsaken or his children begging bread." This verse became alive in me, it became the Rhema word, and I proclaimed it with my mouth many times, in a loud voice, taking authority over the enemy in the Name of Jesus, and stating clearly that the Word I believed was God's and not his. I experienced a relief and a release from that tormenting spirit! Praise the Lord for the power of His Word! I have continued from that day to proclaim God's Word against the tactics and the schemes of the evil one, knowing that "he who is in you is greater than he who is in the world" (1 John 4:4).

The confession and proclamation of the Word of God is also important in reference to the angels. Psalm 103:20 says "Bless the Lord, O you his angels, you mighty ones who do his word, hearkening to the voice of his word!" In other words, the angels are released on our behalf as the Word of God comes out of our mouths; not when we grumble, complain, whine and start confessing negativity! We bind them when we respond like that. Apart from the Word, they won't move; this is one more reason to allow the Holy Spirit to train us in this kind of faith! The ministry of angels exists for our good; "Are they not all ministering spirits sent forth to serve, for the sake of those who are to obtain salvation?" (Hebrews 1:14). If you are a child of God, understand that as you pray the Word for your needs, ministering angels will be released on your behalf! Every morning when I wake up, I plead the Blood of Jesus upon my entire family and over our cars; I ask the Lord to send forth His angels for our protection and to surround our cars. Recently, my son Victor went surfing in Miami Beach; when he finished and went to get his car, the car was gone! Stolen! When Victor called and told me what had happened, I kept reminding the Lord that early in the morning I had covered Victor's car with the Blood of Jesus, and that angels had been released on his behalf; I kept pleading with the Lord for the next ten days that I knew the car had been under His protection and to release His angels to get the car, since the angels are here to help "those who are to obtain salvation!" On the tenth day the car was found in good shape; money and clothes were missing, but the car itself was o.k. I thanked the Lord, for I knew that His angels were responsible for the safe return of the car. Thank you, Jesus!

MORE ON THE WORD

Ps. 119:103 "How sweet are thy words to my taste, sweeter than honey to my mouth."

I cannot say enough about the Word of God. Without it we cannot grow spiritually. God has been more than gracious in giving us His Word, which reveals His Will. Now that we have been transferred from the dominion of darkness to God's kingdom (Colossians 1:13), we need to learn the ways of this new kingdom, and this includes talking and speaking and acting like King Jesus. 2 Timothy 3:16 says that "All scripture is inspired by God and profitable for teaching, for reproof, for correction, and for training in righteousness, that the man of God may be complete, equipped for every good work." In order to become mature and be able to serve our God effectively; in order to be transformed into the image of Christ; in order to evangelize (which is the mission of the Church) we need the Word of God. It simply cannot be done apart from the Word, for it is God's Word that brings life and truth. Salvation does not take place apart from the gospel, for "it is the power of God for salvation to every one who has faith...." (Romans 1:16). People need to hear the Word of truth, the good news of the gospel, in order to repent of their sins and turn to Jesus; someone has to tell them! Why is it this way? Because "it pleased God through the folly of what we preach to save those who believe." (1 Corinthians 1:21b). It's our responsibility to share the gospel with all; this is God's will, because He "desires all men to be saved and to come to the knowledge of the truth." (1 Timothy 2:4). You and I are supposed to share this truth with all, because the Lord does not want that even one person perish. Sharing and preaching the Gospel of Jesus Christ, the message of salvation, is really proclaiming words that bring life. In Mark 16:15, Jesus told his followers to "preach the gospel to the whole creation." Little people like you and I have been given this incredible privilege and responsibility of being able to bring people into God's kingdom through the sharing of the gospel message. This is really using our tongue for life!

The Word of God is so powerful, that I would like to share some of the ways in which it helps us to grow in holiness and become more Christ-like:

–God's words are spirit and life (John 6:63). "It is the spirit that gives life, the flesh is of no avail; the words that I have spoken to you are spirit and life."

–They are like a seed. Mark 4. There will be good fruit coming from the seed of the Word.

–They are like a lamp and light. (Ps.119:105). They bring needed revelation. Because light is more powerful than darkness, the darkness has to flee when the light comes in.

–They are like a hammer and a fire. (Jeremiah 23:29). They tear down strongholds and every proud thing that exalts itself against the Lordship of Jesus Christ; (2 Cor. 10:4-5); fire purifies.

–They will never pass away. (Matthew 24:35). You can stand on this!

–They are sweet as honey. (Ezekiel 3:3). They have the power to transform us and drive out the garbage out of our system and bring sweetness into our lives.

–They keep us from sin. (Ps.119:11). They tell us what pleases and displeases the Lord.

–They strengthen us. (Ps.119:28). They are power-packed!

–They revive us. (Ps.119:25). They have resurrection power!

–They make us wise. (Ps.119:98). They reveal to us the wisdom of God, not the wisdom of the world.

–They give us understanding. (Ps.119:99). We understand now from God's perspective; the eternal perspective.

–They give us peace. (Ps.119:165). Because we know He is in control!

–They counsel us. (P.119:24). They give us the only advice that counts.

–They comfort us. (Ps.119:50). You don't need pills, drugs, or alcohol; the Word will meet you at the point of your need.

–They are like water that washes us. (Ephesians 5:26). We need to be cleansed daily.

–They are like a mirror. (James 1:23). They show us where we fall short, so that we desire to change.

–They uphold and sustain us. (Hebrews 1:3). The biggest force in the universe.

–They are like rock. (Matthew 7:25). The only solid foundation.

–They become the Sword of the Spirit. (Ephesians 6:17). With it, we defeat the enemy and every evil attack.

–They are life and healing to all our flesh. (Proverbs 4:22). Take them just like medicine and you will see results.

It's up to us to feed on God's word and be transformed so that we can become a people that bring life and blessings to others. Tell me, what is more fruitful from the eternal perspective, to get into the Word and pray the Word, or watch one more T.V. show?

ANGER WILL DERAIL YOU!

Ps. 4:4 "Be angry, but sin not; commune with your own hearts on your beds, and be silent."

Usually, when we are angry and we speak, nasty words come out of our mouths; words packed with bitterness and resentments; insults and curses; bad words that bring death and not life! We would do well to heed the advice of James in Chapter 1:19: "Know this, my beloved brethren. Let every man be quick to hear, slow to speak, slow to anger, for the anger of man does not work the righteousness of God." What is the solution? Verse 21 says ". . . receive with meekness the implanted word, which is able to save your souls." Once again, we are to fill up with the Word and allow it to transform our lives. We also need to get filled with the Holy Spirit. The Holy Spirit gives us self-control: "For God did not give us a spirit of timidity, but a spirit of power and love and self-control." (2 Timothy 1:7). We are not alone in this; our Helper will help us when we call on Him, and He'll help us control our tongues. In Galatians 5:23, we see self-control as the ninth-fold fruit of the Holy Spirit. If you have the Holy Spirit, you have self-control. Learn to release it! Proverbs 15:1 says "A soft answer turns away wrath, but a harsh word stirs up anger." Anger brings about more anger in yourself and others; it's a vicious cycle that needs to be broken. Verse 18 says "A hot-tempered man stirs up strife, but he who is slow to anger quiets contention." When we keep our peace and give a soft answer, contention is ended.

Anger is one of the doorways through which the enemy comes in; this is another reason why we shouldn't stay angry or nurse our anger. Ephesians 4:26-27 says "Be angry, but do not sin; do not let the sun go down on your anger, and give no opportunity to the devil." In other words, we will get angry at times, but don't nurse it! Let it go, especially before the day is over! Forgive that person and release him or her over to the Lord. Anger is an invitation for demonic activity; If you stay angry long enough, you're giving the devil an opportunity to "steal, kill, and destroy" in your life! The enemy comes in with nothing good for you; he might bring depression, fear, sickness, lies and anxiety, just to name some of the garbage that he brings when there's an open door. I know people that are bound by anger; they have no peace in their lives. With their words they kill; later they're sorry, but the harm has been done. In Christ, there's another way to live; He's come to set us free. He's the Truth that sets us free! There is freedom in Christ from that anger! We can actually change our tongues from an instrument of death to an instrument of life, by His grace!

Proverbs 22:24-25 says "Make no friendship with a man given to anger, nor go with a wrathful man, lest you learn his ways and entangle yourself in a snare." I believe you can definitely pick up the bad from people; the saying "a rotten apple spoils the rest" has a lot of truth to it. However, there can also be a transference of evil spirits when ties are formed with angry people. It's obvious in some families that there's a lot of anger in the family tree, and only the Lord Jesus can break that curse and bring freedom and transformation. Jesus is always the solution; He's already dealt with all of our garbage at the Cross and if we repent and ask Him for help, He'll do it.

Recently I was so angry with somebody, and with good reason; I was tempted to call this person back on the telephone and just tell them what a rotten human being this person was. I had, literally, my hand on the phone to make the call; but by God's grace I didn't. Instead, I forgave and released this person to the Lord and asked the Lord to bless this person. I spoke with the Lord and told Him "You are the one that defends me; I don't have to defend myself; I give up my right to prove I was right. I release once again this matter into your hands." About ten minutes later the telephone rang, and behold, it's the same person calling me back, and apologizing! The Holy Spirit Himself, with His convicting power, touched this person! I didn't have to call back in anger to use my tongue in the wrong way; I didn't have to "play God" to convince this person of wrongdoing; when I let go, the Holy Spirit was freed to do His work! The apostle Paul says in Romans 12:21 "Do not be overcome by evil, but overcome evil with good." When we forgive and refuse to give in to anger, we are overcoming evil with good. Praise the Lord!

DONT LET UNFORGIVENESS BLOCK YOU!

Luke 23:34 "And Jesus said, "Father, forgive them, for they know not what they do."

These words from Jesus came as He hung on the Cross; He proclaimed them out loud for all to hear and for them to be kept forever in His Word for all generations to see. This is the heart of Jesus: one of forgiveness! He forgave all of us for having nailed Him to the Cross! Glory to God!

St. Paul says in Ephesians 4:32 "…and be kind to one another, tenderhearted, forgiving one another, as God in Christ forgave you." When the Lord forgives us for our sins, how can we not forgive others their sins against us? In the Our Father, Jesus taught His disciples to pray for forgiveness "as we also have forgiven our debtors" (Matthew 6:12). In other words, our forgiveness is conditional and dependent as to whether we ourselves have forgiven others or not! Jesus goes on to say in verses 14 and 15 "For if you forgive men their trespasses, your heavenly Father also will forgive you; but if you do not forgive men their trespasses, neither will your Father forgive your trespasses." It's your choice to forgive and be forgiven, or to not forgive and not be forgiven!

Our relationships are so important to the Lord, that He tells His disciples in the Sermon on the Mount that "if you are offering your gift at the altar, and there remember that your brother has something against you, leave your gift there before the altar and go; first be reconciled to your brother, and then come and offer your gift." (Matthew 5:23-24). Forgiveness is Basic Christianity 101! And there are so many in the Body of Christ with unforgiveness in their hearts! Forgiveness is not an option, but a command from the Lord. It grieves the Holy Spirit!

Do you know how often we must forgive? CONTINUOUSLY! When Peter asked Jesus, "Lord, how often shall my brother sin against me, and I forgive him? As many as seven times? Jesus said to him, "I do not say to you seven times, but seventy times seven." (Matthew 18:21-22).

Unforgiveness has other negative effects in our lives: it opens the door for the enemy to "steal, kill and destroy," and it also hinders our prayer life. In the parable of the Merciless Official, Jesus says that when we don't forgive and we insist on unforgiveness, the master will hand us over to the "torturers." Who are the torturers? Evil spirits assigned to harass, torment, and destroy our lives with sickness, disease, depression, anxiety attacks, and the like. Jesus says that "My heavenly Father will treat you in exactly the same way unless each of you forgives his brother from the heart." (Matthew 18:34-35).

Unforgiveness can also hinder our prayer life. In Mark 11:25, Jesus says, "And whenever you stand praying, forgive, if you have anything against anyone; so that your Father also who is in heaven may forgive you your trespasses." Have you not received answers to your prayers? Check your heart and make sure you have forgiven everyone who has ever hurt you.

In short, forgiveness is a command from God; it pleases God; it's continuous (by His grace); frees the Holy Spirit to flow in our lives; brings healing into our hearts and bodies; allows God to forgive us.

On the other hand, unforgiveness causes your own sins not to be forgiven; hinders your prayer life; grieves the Holy Spirit; and opens the door for the enemy to come and torment us. Where do you want to go with your life? If you don't forgive you will not advance!

I believe that many who are reading this book have not forgiven from the heart and are still holding anger, grudges and resentment; if you are one of them, I ask you to say this prayer out loud, with your tongue: (the enemy has to hear you).

"Heavenly Father, I come before you in the name of Jesus to forgive every person who has ever harmed me (Ask the Holy Spirit to reveal who these people are). I ask you for the grace that I need right now to forgive them; I can't do it on my own, but with your grace I can. I forgive_____ and release them unto your care for You to bless them. I release all anger, bitterness, resentment and rage; I don't want to carry them any longer! Fill my heart with your Holy Spirit; fill me with your peace, joy and love. I'm free! Thank you, Jesus! Satan, in the name of Jesus, you cannot harass or torment me any longer; I'm a child of God, redeemed from your hand by the Blood of Jesus. Get out of my life in the name of Jesus!"

IT'S YOUR CHOICE TO CROSS THE JORDAN!

Jesus came that we may "have life, and have it abundantly." It is God's desire that we experience His life in this planet! The Apostle Paul says in Romans 14:17 that the kingdom of God is "righteousness, peace and joy in the Holy Spirit." He wants us to experience His peace and joy, His provision and kindness, His power, healing and deliverance, and of course, His forgiveness and His saving power CONTINUOUSLY! Ps. 103:2 says to "forget not all his benefits." Some of His benefits include forgiveness of our sins (which already took place in the Cross 2,000 years ago through the shedding of His Blood); healing of all our diseases (He also carried our diseases at Calvary); His redemption, His steadfast love and mercy, His provision so that we can be satisfied with good, and renewing power to make us and keep us strong. These are some of His benefits.

The Lord also wants us to experience His power working in us and through us. He has given us the spiritual weapons that we need in order to overcome the flesh, the world and the devil, all stemming from His glorious victory at the Cross of Calvary. He has given us the powerful Name of Jesus, at which name everything and everyone has to bow. He has given us the Blood of Jesus, the Holy Spirit, and His Word.

The enemy comes to "steal, kill, and destroy" (John 10:10) everything in our lives, but "He who is in you is greater than he who is in the world." (1 John 4:4). Just think of how awesome is this Word: the God of the universe indwells every believer, and is more powerful than all the human and satanic strategy that has been sent our way. Alleluia! Our adversary, the devil, certainly, does not want us to experience the abundant life that Jesus came to give us, and he will try and try and try to steal it from us. But we have power and authority in the Name of Jesus and by the power of His precious Blood, to "tread upon serpents and scorpions, and over all the power of the enemy ...." (Luke 10:19).

Just like the Israelites had to cross the River Jordan to "possess the land," We must cross over from unbelief to belief so that we can "possess the promised life." We make a choice to leave the world behind and not allow the flesh to control us. God's people walk by faith, not by sight; this means that we keep our focus on the Lord Jesus and His promises, not on our circumstances. This means that we walk by revelation, that we trust His Word and rely in the Lord completely, not allowing our emotions to control us; it's the Holy Spirit who is now guiding us!

It's through "faith and patience that we inherit the promises." (Hebrews 6:12). Just as the Lord opened the River Jordan for Joshua and the Israelites, He will open the way for us and our families. We need to believe and walk in faith, believing that every promise of God in the Scriptures is for us today.

The way we use our tongue is crucial! Remember James' word that our tongue is like a bit in a horse's mouth and like the rudder of a ship; depending on how we use it we will or will not make it to our destiny. It is God's perfect will that we make it. If we keep grumbling, complaining and murmuring, we will keep on lapping around in circles going nowhere! Let's cooperate with Him! His grace is available for us!

The Lord gave Joshua good advice before entering the Promised Land. I believe these words are as good for us today as they were for Joshua and company thousands of years ago. We need to be "doers of the Word" in order to take over the "promised life" and the blessings that the Lord won for us in Calvary. In the Book of Joshua 1:7-8 it says "Only be strong and courageous, being careful to do according to all the law which Moses my servant commanded you; turn not from it to the right hand or to the left, that you may have good success wherever you go. This book of the law SHALL NOT DEPART OUT OF YOUR MOUTH, but you shall meditate on it day and night, that you may be careful to do according to all that is written in it; for then you shall make your way prosperous, and then you shall have good success." Do you see the relationship between always having the Word of God in our mouths, always meditating on it, and obedience to the Lord? For the Jewish people, meditating is much more than a mental exercise; it involves repetition of the words.

Are you ready for a new life in this planet? Are you ready to leave behind old sinful habits and lifestyles that have gotten you nowhere? Are you willing to smash your idols? Are you ready to surrender your tongue to the Holy Spirit? Are you desirous that the Lord Jesus be glorified in your life? Do you want to experience the abundant life? Do you want to become an instrument of blessing? Do you want to be used powerfully by God? Do you want more of the Holy Spirit?

LET'S PRAY: *Holy Spirit, I surrender my life to you. Like Mary, I say today "Let it be done to me according to your Word." Guide me, teach me, show me the way. I give up my sin, my stubbornness, my rebellion, my idolatry, my blindness and deafness. I surrender my tongue to you. Come and start a new work in me; give me what I need to walk in victory. I give you permission to work in me and through me. I want Jesus to be exalted and glorified in my life. Give me a great hunger for the Word of God. Holy Spirit, come and fill me, baptize me with your fire. I'm ready; I want it. Thank you, Jesus!*

TAKE OUT YOUR SWORD AND FIGHT!

As mentioned before, the Word of God is the Sword of the Spirit as it becomes rhema, or alive, in our hearts. This is the sword of victory, this word of truth full of light and power to overcome darkness and evil. No demon power can withstand the power and authority of this Word. No wonder the devil has convinced so many Catholics that it is not that important to know the Word; it is a "protestant thing." That's why so many believers are in defeat and going around in circles, never experiencing the rest and victory of the Lord. We have many battles to fight (Ephesians 6:10-18) because the enemy of our souls comes to attack. Peter says in 1 Peter 5:8 "Be sober, be watchful. Your adversary the devil prowls around like a roaring lion, seeking some one to devour." If you are asleep in the pew of the church, wake up before the enemy "steals, kills and destroys" everything in your life!

Our model is Jesus in the desert as He was being tempted by satan (Matthew 4). Every time the enemy came to tempt Him, how did Jesus defend Himself? He quoted from the Word of God, and that sword of the spirit came out in power and force; the devil had to leave. Three times Jesus answered "for it is written" and proclaimed the Word of God.

Brothers and sisters, we are children of God, and the Lord has given us power and authority over the devil. He has already been defeated at the Cross (Colossians 2:14-15); however, he's still alive; he's a defeated foe and WE NEED TO TAKE AUTHORITY OVER HIM AND KICK HIM OUT OF OUR LIVES AND THE LIVES OF OUR CHILDREN! We are to "submit to God, resist the devil, and he will flee from you." (James 4:7). This means that we must walk in obedience to God and His Word, submitted to the Lordship of Jesus Christ; in this position we resist the devil and command him to leave in Jesus' name. We have him under our feet (Ephesians 2:6), and he knows it! He also knows that "He who is in us, is greater than he who is in the world." (1 John 4:4). He has to flee! Resist him!

1 John 3:5 says "You know that he appeared to take away sins . . ." and 1John 3:8 says ". . . The reason the Son of God appeared

was to destroy the works of the devil."

All Christians are in agreement that on the Cross, Jesus Christ, the Lamb of God, took away the sins of the world. But let's not stop there; let Him destroy the works of the devil in our lives and the lives of our children. The works of the devil are many: sin, death, curses, poverty, addiction, division, strife, shame, sickness and disease, lies and deceit, learning disabilities, fear and panic attacks, just to name a few. Many Christians are just content to receive forgiveness of their sins, and of course, that's the most important! But that's not all that Jesus did and wants to do for us. There's more! There's the abundant life: a life in fellowship with our God and with our brothers and sisters; a life marked by joy, love, and peace; a life where we experience God's saving and healing power; a life where we experience His blessings over every area of our lives; a life where we experience victory over sin and satan and over every evil attack.

The Word of God needs to be proclaimed over every situation and difficulty we might be experiencing. Remember, there's a promise in Scripture for any difficulty, for any adversity, for any lack, for any disease that we might be facing. The enemy can't come against the Word of God and he knows it. Let's bring life and victory into these situations by the proclamation of the Word and not by proclaiming negativity, doubt, unbelief, grumbling and complaining. When we live according to the Word and we proclaim the Word, we crush the enemy; it's like crushing a cockroach. He thinks he's "a roaring lion" but he's more like a toothless dog! Amen!

We walk by faith and not by sight; the world walks by sight. Our trust and our dependence is on the Lord and on His promises. Ps 149:4 says "For the Lord takes pleasure in his people; He adorns the humble with victory." As we wait on the Lord with a humble dependence, sooner or later we will be "adorned with victory!" Our God is dependable; He is trustworthy; if He has said it in His Word, we believe it and we stand on that rock. This is why it's so important to know the promises of our God; if we don't know them, we might perish for "lack of knowledge." (Hosea 4:6)

When in trouble, pray the Word in the name of Jesus, and ask the Holy Spirit to give you a "fresh word" (manna) for that specific situation. Trust me, He's going to give it to you. God is more interested in your welfare than you are! Recently, I experienced the enemy's attack regarding my children's future. The "word" the Lord gave me was from Ps. 20:7, which says "Some trust in horses, some trust in chariots, but I trust in the name of the Lord my God." (NIV). I was led to repeat this verse throughout the night over and over again, until I experienced a release from the Holy Spirit. Verse six says "Now I know that the Lord will help his anointed; He will answer him from his holy heaven with mighty victories by His right hand." Alleluia! I did experience a victory in that situation, but not right away; it was several months before I saw it with my eyes, but nevertheless, God had given me His Word, and I just kept praising and thanking Him in advance until I had the victory in my hand! I stood on His Word without wavering. Only the Holy Spirit can enable us to live like this.

When the Holy Spirit anoints a passage of Scripture, grab it, take it, store it in your heart, memorize it, proclaim it! You will be proclaiming life over what is facing you. It's yours! Don't let it fall on the ground, but proclaim it (with your mouth; out loud), as the Sword of the Spirit.

The enemy comes to lie. The battleground is our mind. It's our choice to believe the enemy's lies or the truth of the Word of God. Whose report will you believe? What usually happens is that the devil puts negative thoughts in our minds and we repeat those lies again and again and again; we think it's our thoughts, when in reality we have been listening to the enemy and what we have been confessing with our mouths are his lies. As we repeat his negative thoughts, "I'll never make it;" "I'll never get healed;" "There's no way out;" "Nobody loves me;" "I can't make it;" "God doesn't care about me;" etc., we are confessing and proclaiming death and not life. We need discernment to understand what's taking place in our lives, and rise up and take authority over the devil, taking "every thought captive to obey Christ,..." (2 Corinthians 10:5). Many times we are under "attack", and we don't even know it. My daughter Rosario, a student at Villanova University, was having a rough time during finals her freshman year. She had to study, read and write several papers within a short time. She was overwhelmed and stressed out, and called me and started crying over the phone. She was saying exactly what the enemy wanted her to say (remember there's power in the spoken word, for good or bad); "I won't be able to make it;" "I'm too upset;" "I don't think I'm smart;" etc. I had to bind in the name of Jesus the evil spirits of self-pity, discouragement, negativity, confusion and any spirit that wasn't the Holy Spirit, and we started to pray the opposite; we asked the Holy Spirit to take control of the situation and to fill her with peace and joy. We praised and thanked God for His sufficient grace and I had her repeat words of life. I cancelled the effects of every negative word she had spoken, in the name of Jesus, and when we hung up she was a different person. She was able to work things out!

Phillipians 1:6 "And I am sure that he who began a good work in you will bring it to completion...."

POWER IN PRAISE!

Ps.145: "My mouth will speak the praise of the Lord, and let all flesh bless his holy name for ever and ever."

It was only when I got baptized with the Holy Spirit, that I praised the Lord Jesus for the first time in my life. This was something new in my life; clearly the work of the Holy Spirit, whose main function is to point to Jesus and glorify Him. (John16:14). 1 Corinthians 12:3 says "...no one can say that Jesus is Lord except by the Holy Spirit." It's the Holy Spirit that reveals and magnifies Jesus and causes praise to flow from us. Praising the Lord is not a sing-a-long nor a songfest; it is the very reason we have been created (1 Peter 2:9) and it ushers in the very presence of God. Ps. 22:3 says that the Lord is "enthroned on the praises of Israel." Let's get to the point: Praises bring in the manifest presence of God, and when He comes, He comes to bless His people. Our praises invite Him, and when He comes, He comes to heal, deliver, save, restore; He comes to speak and to move His powerful right arm in our midst. As He dwells in the midst of our praise, the darkness is dispelled. The Holy Spirit wants to keep on doing exactly the same things Jesus did when He walked on earth; "...He went about doing good and healing all that were oppressed by the devil, for God was with Him." (Acts 10:38).

Let's go back to Ps. 22. Let's look at verse 4: "In thee our fathers trusted; they trusted and thou didst deliver them. To thee they cried, and were saved; in thee they trusted, and were not disappointed." There's deliverance, salvation and no disappointment in the presence of the Lord! There's also freedom and transformation in the Presence of the Lord. 2 Corinthians 3:17-18 says that "Now the Lord is the Spirit, and where the Spirit of the Lord is, there is freedom. And we all, with unveiled face, beholding the glory of the Lord, are being changed into his likeness from one degree of glory to another; for this comes from the Lord who is the Spirit." You want to grow in holiness and be changed and transformed into the image of Jesus Christ? Spend time in His presence, praising and worshipping Him! We gaze at Him, not at ourselves! We can spend years in a psychiatrist's couch looking at ourselves without any real transformation; but with the Holy Spirit it's a different story; He's the transformer, the One that changes us and makes us whole. And all this takes place in His presence, brought about by our praise and worship. When we praise the Lord, we give Him a platform to work from. This is really using our tongue as an instrument of life and blessing!

One Saturday when we were in jail, praising and worshipping the Lord, there was a tremendous anointing, an incredible presence in the room. I saw the Lord Jesus standing in front of one of the inmates; she was deeply touched and weeping. When we stopped praising and worshipping Jesus, I said to her, "Sister, I saw the Lord Jesus standing in front of you." She answered that indeed she had felt His presence, "but all I know is that I walked in here with a lump in my breast and now it's gone!" The Lord gave us that day a little touch of the great things He wants to do in our lives, but He shows up where He's wanted. In the great year of the Jubilee 2,000, as four of us praised the Lord in "spirit and in truth," my friend's lump in her hand disappeared as we laid our hands on it and commanded it to disappear. In my parish of St. Louis (Miami), at the charismatic prayer group, a lady who for 18 long years had suffered from tremendous pain in her back due to a car accident, was suddenly set free from the pain in that atmosphere of praise as we laid hands on her. She's still free!

Hebrews 13:15 "Through Him then let us continually offer up a sacrifice of praise to God, that is, the fruit of lips that acknowledge his name." Praise is to be offered up to God continually! That means at all times, even when we don't feel like it! Praise becomes a sacrifice at such times. I believe that praise is intended to "kill" the flesh. It's God's remedy so that we can get out of our negative feelings and emotions as we make a choice to leave ourselves behind and move towards Him. When we praise God, we leave "self" behind. We move out of our anger, fear, anxiety, self-pity, resentments, sadness, hurts and pains, and into God. In the most painful times of my life, as I have faced the pain of abandonment and rejection and the trauma of a broken home, it has been in His presence that I have been progressively healed and restored.

It's our choice to remain bound by the flesh or to enter into His presence with thanksgiving and praise (Ps. 100) and be changed and freed. The biggest hindrance to praising the Lord is self; "I'm too sad;" "I'm too depressed;" "I'm too sick;" "I'm too miserable;" "I don't feel like it;" "I'm too worried;" It's at precisely such times that we need to praise the Lord more than ever, because it's in His presence that we are changed, and praise releases the Lord's powerful right arm to move on our behalf. We praise God always because of Who He is and because He is worthy of all our praise and adoration; He's still seated at the throne, no matter what we're going through! It's precisely when praise becomes a sacrifice that it's very pleasing in the eyes of God. Ps 69:30-31 says "I will praise the name of God with a song; I will magnify him with thanksgiving. This will please the Lord MORE than an ox or a bull with horns and hoofs." It's wonderful to praise God during the good times, but it's especially pleasing to Him when we praise Him during the "bad times." Instead of grumbling, complaining and getting angry, which lead to nowhere, our praise becomes a very pleasing sacrifice in His eyes. What a way to use our tongue! We're ushering in the very atmosphere of heaven, which is one of praise and worship; and in this kind of atmosphere great things happen. In this kind of atmosphere the Holy Spirit is free to move and do what He wills.

Praising the Lord is also a great weapon against the enemy. Wherever the name of Jesus is lifted up, the enemy has to flee; he can't take it! When we praise the name of Jesus, we're placing Him in the highest place, far above any problem, difficulty, worry or anxiety. He's bigger, much bigger, than any circumstance. In the Book of Acts 16, there's a powerful story about how Paul and Silas started to sing and praise the Lord while imprisoned. Instead of complaining and whining (like most of us would do), they did the opposite. Verse 25 says "About midnight (the darkest moment in our lives), Paul and Silas were praying and singing hymns to God…" Then, something amazing happened; "Suddenly there was a great earthquake, so that the foundations of the prison were shaken; and immediately all the doors were opened and everyone's fetters were unfastened." (v.26). POWERFUL! Everyone in that prison experienced deliverance! Doors that needed to be opened got opened! Chains broke loose! I want to tell you that if you have the Holy Spirit you have the power of dynamite inside of you to cause many earthquakes through praise and worship. Praise the Lord! What a way to use our tongue! Expect great things in the midst of praise and worship.

Let's go to 2 Chronicles 20, in the Old Testament. This is another powerful praise story. The king of Judah and Jerusalem was going to be attacked by three armies more powerful than his. Some men came and told the King that "A great multitude is coming against you . . ." Sometimes we feel that our problems are so overwhelming that we can't possibly overcome them. Of course, on our own we can't, but with the help of the Holy Spirit we can. The Word says that "we are more than conquerors through Him who loved us." (Romans 8:37). The king sought the Lord, proclaimed a fast and assembled the people to pray. In verse 12 he tells God "...For we are powerless against this great multitude that is coming against us. We do not know what to do, but our eyes are upon thee." Right here starts the victory: when we proclaim our dependence on the Lord and take our eyes off the circumstances and place our eyes upon the Lord. When we look at Jesus, words of praise is what comes out of our mouths, for He is worthy! When we focus on the difficulty, negativity is what comes out of us; (we saw that with the Israelites). In the midst of this prayer assembly, the Holy Spirit spoke through one of His prophets an incredible Word: "Thus says the Lord to you, fear not, and be not dismayed at this great multitude; for the battle is not yours but God's." Powerful!!! It continues (v.17) with "You will not need to fight in this battle; take your position, stand still, and see the victory of the Lord on your behalf, O Judah and Jerusalem. Fear not, and be not dismayed; tomorrow go out against them, and the Lord will be with you." In our own lives the battle belongs to the Lord too, but we still need to take our position and face the enemy. The Lord will do the fighting on our behalf. Our position is one of standing upon the rock of His Word, thanking, praising and worshipping Him. Let's continue; the king and his people worshipped and praised the Lord and on the morning of the battle the king placed "the choir" at the head of the army, not the best trained warriors! The praisers went before the army singing "Give thanks to the Lord, for his steadfast love endures forever." (v.21). As the army sang and praised God, God himself set ambushes in the enemy camp. The three enemy armies got confused and destroyed each other. God's people didn't even lose one man! As God's people praised the Lord, the Lord Himself got rid of their enemies! See the power of praise?

When you are facing difficulties on every side, how do you respond? When someone in your family gets sick, how do you respond? If your children are hanging out with the "wrong crowd," how do you respond? If your child comes home with an "F," how do you respond? If you find your children are using drugs, how do you respond? If your spouse is having an affair, how do you respond? If you get fired from your job, how do you respond? If you are having problems with your in-laws, how do you respond? In the flesh, the natural thing would be to start grumbling, complaining, cursing and getting angry. BUT WE HAVE THE HOLY SPIRIT WITH US, TO HELP US RESPOND IN A DIFFERENT WAY, IN A GODLY WAY! We need to respond in faith and start thanking the Lord and praising His Holy Name. This frees the Holy Spirit to move and work things out. Once, when my son Ricky was not allowed to participate in his senior retreat because he paid the retreat fee one day late, I was very disappointed, to say the least; probably out of that senior class he was the best candidate for it! Naturally, I called the school, but they would not make an exception for Ricky. I started to thank the Lord in advance, knowing that there would be a better retreat for him. Three weeks later Ricky did go on retreat; the Lord touched his heart and even wrote me a letter saying that he was sorry for being a brat and that he loved me even though he didn't tell me every day! I found out later that the senior retreat had been a disaster and cancelled and the kids sent home. The Lord always honors our faith. Thank you, Jesus!

Psalm 149 is an awesome Word about high praise and its powerful effects in our surroundings. Basically, what it says is that as we touch the Lord with our praises, demonic power is bound and pushed out of the way. The last verse says that "This is glory for all his faithful ones." In 1996, during an evangelistic outreach in my native country of Cuba, we experienced the power of praise in a dramatic way. We were staying in the old section of Havana, in a fourth story, overlooking a small plaza. Every night in that plaza we saw the young prostitutes selling their bodies to the tourists; we saw a lot of drinking and carrying on. The noise continued every night into the early morning. One night, without any prior planning, we started to praise the Lord with some Mexican musicians; we praised until 3:00 a.m. Our praises spilled out of a huge window overlooking the plaza; across the street we saw people in balconies kneeling and praying and worshipping the Lord. Some had their hands outstretched to the Lord. It was an awesome sight! The next night there was so much quiet and peace in the plaza, that we were struck by it. Then we realized that the Lord had used our praises to move the evil forces over that area out of the way. Thank you, Jesus! Do you realize that the atmosphere in our homes, work places, neighborhoods, cities and nations can actually be changed through our tongues? We must remember that we do not battle against flesh and blood, but against demonic powers in the heavenlies (Ephesians 6:12), and praise is used by God to drive out the enemy. Let's use our tongues to drive the enemy forces out of our lives! Tell me, have the government programs been successful against violence, abuse, immorality, crime? It's time to take God at His Word, believing that as we praise Him our praises become "two-edged swords in our hands" (Ps. 149:6) that overcome and bind the enemy. We need spiritual weapons to overcome our spiritual enemies, and praise is one of those weapons!

The Lord Jesus Himself came out of the tribe of Judah, which means "praise." It was the tribe of Judah that led the Israelites in the desert (Numbers 2:3,9). This means that praising the Lord goes first; just as in Chronicles 20. It's our first response, no matter what is happening in our lives. Only with the help of the Holy Spirit can we live like this. Remember the grumbling, complaining, and the negativity of the Israelites in the desert! They kept going in circles for forty years and never entered into their destiny!

POWER IN THE SHOUT!

Ps. 35:27-28 "Let those who desire my vindication shout for joy and be glad, and say evermore, "Great is the Lord, who delights in the welfare of his servant!"

There's power in the shout, when we are supposed to shout. There are times in our lives that the Holy Spirit leads us to shout; there are shouts of joy, shouts of victory, shouts of praise, shouts for help and battle shouts. Those walls in your life will come tumbling down, just like the walls of Jericho. The walls around Jericho came tumbling down as Joshua obeyed the Word of the Lord and the entire nation of Israel shouted in unison, at the precise moment. (Joshua 6:20). Blind Bartimeaus cried out to Jesus and kept on shouting and received his healing (Mark 10:47-48); Peter cried out to the Lord as he was sinking and the Lord saved him (Matthew 14:30-31); the ten lepers in Luke 17:13 "lifted up their voices and said, Jesus, Master, have mercy on us." They were healed! In the same story the Samaritan that returned to thank Jesus, praised God "with a loud voice" (v.15), and he received the "double cure" of healing and salvation! In John 11:43, Jesus "cried with a loud voice, Lazarus, come out. The dead man came out …." During the Visitation, Luke 1:41-42, when Elizabeth was filled with the Holy Spirit, she exclaimed with a loud cry "Blessed are you among women, and blessed is the fruit of your womb!" During Palm Sunday, as Jesus was entering Jerusalem, "the entire crowd of disciples began to rejoice and praise God loudly for the display of power they had seen…" The Pharisees got upset and told Jesus, "Teacher, rebuke your disciples." He replied, "If they were to keep silence, I tell you the very stones would cry out." (Luke 19:37-40). (NAB). My dear brothers and sisters, are we going to let the stones cry out, or are we going to "shout" our praises to the living God? It's time to get a little "undignified," to become fools for Jesus. Dignity is not a fruit of the Holy Spirit!

Jesus is a shouting man of war. Isaiah 42:13 says "The Lord goes forth like a mighty man, like a man of war he stirs up his fury; he cries out, he shouts aloud, he shows himself mighty against his foes." When we are in the midst of spiritual warfare, and we shout in unison with the Lord, great deliverances and healings take place. Recently I was ministering at a Healing Crusade in St. Petersburg, Fl., and as we all shouted in unison to Jesus, there were healings in our midst that took place; people were set free from arthritis, migraines and depression; broken hearts were healed and the joy of the Lord was released. Everyone experienced a touch from the Lord!

Numbers 23:21b says "The Lord their God is with them, and the shout of a king is among them." He is the captain of the army, and when He shouts, we do the same. The Lord gave Gideon the victory as his army cried in unison "A sword for the Lord and for Gideon." (Judges 7:20). My son Eddy experienced the power of God as he cried out at the top of his lungs when his friend almost drowned and had no pulse nor heart beat when they took him out of the water. They started doing First Aid, but in the meantime Eddy kept shouting "Lord, don't let him die!" "You will not die, you will live;" "Jesus, save him!" What my son was really doing was prophesying and speaking life over his friend! In a moment of desperation, he was not ashamed to call on Jesus at the top of his lungs in front of others. His friend is alive and well, with no brain damage! Thank you, Jesus!

Many people that shout and scream their lungs out at football games are so "dignified" and "respectable" when it comes to shouting praises unto the Lord! But to us belongs the victory shout! Salvation is worth shouting about! Jesus is worth shouting about! Not only that, He is a shouting King, and when He comes back, He's coming with a shout or "a cry of command." (1 Thessalonians 4:16).

When we shout out to Jesus and proclaim His name, great things happen in the invisible world, because the name of Jesus is the key that opens heaven, and is the name above all other names; at His name "every knee must bow" (Phil.2:9) and everything that has a name has to submit to the name of Jesus; our spiritual enemies (depression, fear, anxiety, etc.) have to flee at His name. Years ago, when my daughter Rosario was about nine years old, we were vacationing in a private little island in the Bahamas. My daughter suffered a very nasty cut in one of her fingers and there was not a doctor in the island, but we had Doctor Jesus! Immediately I wrapped her finger with a towel and started to pray. Without hesitation, my daughter started to cry out and shout to Jesus asking for healing. "Jesus, Jesus, Jesus, please heal my finger!" A few minutes later, I took off the towel and her finger was healed; there was only the slightest scar! Praise God!

Here are a few "shouting" verses:

Ps. 20:5 "May we shout for joy over your victory, and in the name of our God set up our banners!"

Ps. 27:6-7 "And now my head shall be lifted up above my enemies round about me; and I will offer in his tent sacrifices with shouts of joy; I will sing and make melody to the Lord. Hear, O Lord, when I cry aloud, be gracious to me and answer me."

Ps. 33:3 "Sing to Him a new song, play skillfully on the strings, with loud shouts."

Ps. 32:11 "Be glad in the Lord, and rejoice, O righteous, and shout for joy, all you upright in heart!

Ps. 47:1 "Clap your hands, all peoples! Shout to God with loud songs of joy."

Ps. 78: 65-66 "Then the Lord awoke as from sleep, like a strong man shouting because of wine. And he put his adversaries to rout: he put them to everlasting shame."

Ps. 89:15 "Blessed are the people who know the festal shout, who walk, O Lord, in the light of thy countenance..."

Ps. 118:15 "The joyful shout of victory in the tents of the just; The right hand of the Lord has struck with power ..." (NAB).

Ps. 126:5-6 "May those who sow in tears reap with shouts of joy! He that goes forth weeping, bearing the seed for sowing, shall come home with shouts of joy, bringing his sheaves with him."

Rev. 19:6 "Then I heard what sounded like the shouts of a great crowd, or the roaring of the deep, or mighty peals of thunder, as they cried: Alleluia! The Lord is King, our God, the Almighty!"

2 Chronicles 13:15 "Then the men of Judah raised the battle shout. And when the men of Judah shouted, God defeated Jeroboam and all Israel before Abijah and Judah."

2 Chronicles 15:14 "They took oath to the Lord with a loud voice, and with shouting, and with trumpets, and with horns."

Tell me, friend, isn't Jesus worth shouting about? If you were sinking and there was nobody around to help you, except Jesus, wouldn't you shout for Him to help you?

THERE ARE TIMES TO BE SILENT!

Ps. 46:10 "Be still and know that I am God…"

As God's people, we are guided by the Holy Spirit, and there will be times when we are not supposed to say anything. We must develop a "listening ear" to hear what the Holy Spirit wants to tell us. Prayer is communication with our God, and it's supposed to be two-way! At other times we will have to exercise self-control with others by not saying anything, even though we may want to. This, of course, is really "taming" our tongue! James says in chapter 3:8 "…but no human being can tame the tongue—a restless evil, full of deadly poison." Only when we give the Holy Spirit our tongue will it be controlled.

When Joshua was ready to lead the Israelites into the Promised Land, after forty years of going around in circles, He gave them strict orders as to how things were going to be done. In Joshua 6:10, Joshua tells them: "You shall not shout or let your voice be heard, neither shall any word go out of your mouth, until the day I bid you shout; then you shall shout." In other words, Joshua was telling them to keep quiet; no comments, no opinions, no discussion, until it was time to "shout" those walls down. He probably remembered very well what had happened forty years earlier, and now he didn't want to take any chances!

James 3:2 says "For we all make many mistakes, and if any one makes no mistakes in what he says he is a perfect man, able to bridle the whole body also." When our tongue is under control, our entire body will be under control as well, because the tongue is like a bridle that keeps us controlled. We have two great examples in the Bible in Jesus and Mary of how they kept their tongues under control and kept their peace in very difficult situations. The silence of Jesus during the Passion says more than a million words. He must have been under tremendous temptation to use His tongue to defend Himself and to condemn, criticize and insult others; but He didn't! Read carefully what Peter says in 1 Peter 3:22-23: "He committed no sin; no guile was found on his lips. When he was reviled, he did not revile in return; when he suffered he did not threaten; but He trusted to Him who judges justly." Jesus had his tongue under control; His trust was placed on His Father totally and absolutely and had no need to defend Himself with His tongue. We, His followers, are called to follow in His footsteps! Peter says in verse 21 "For to this you have been called, because Christ also suffered for you, leaving you an example, that you should follow in His steps." We are called to follow Jesus in this way; not use our tongue as an instrument of death, even when it is to our "disadvantage"! Our God is in control and He takes care of His own; we can trust Him because "we know that in everything God works for good with those who love him...." (Romans 8:28). When Mary of Bethany anointed Jesus with very costly ointment and His disciples criticized her, Mary did not open her mouth, and Jesus took care of defending her. Jesus told them "Let her alone; why do you trouble her? She has done a beautiful thing to me." (Mark 14:6). Jesus was so pleased with Mary's display of love for Him that in verse nine Jesus says: "Truly, I say to you, wherever the gospel is preached in the whole world, what she has done will be told in memory of her." The prophet Isaiah says in chapter 53:7: "He was oppressed, and He was afflicted, yet He opened not His mouth; like a lamb that is led to the slaughter, and like a sheep that before its shearers is dumb, so He opened not His mouth." Thank you, Jesus, that you did not sin with your tongue!

Mother Mary was one that kept her tongue under control. Unlike the Israelites in the desert, who grumbled, complained and whined every step of the way, Mary kept her peace and did not use her tongue in an ungodly way. She kept quiet during very difficult circumstances: when Joseph was ready to divorce her; when at nine months pregnant she had to journey to Bethlehem; when there was no room at the inn; when Jesus was lost for three days; when Jesus didn't leave the crowd to come to talk to her; and last, but not least, she is silent as she stands by her crucified Son at the Cross. How in the world could she respond so docilely and with such self-control to so much adversity? How could she control her tongue as she saw her beloved Son being despised, mocked and crucified? She knew her God! She knew the meaning of Romans 8:28!

CALL THE THINGS THAT ARE NOT

Romans 4:17 ". . . who gives life to the dead and calls into existence the things that do not exist."

Because we walk by faith, with our eyes fixed on Jesus and on His promises, we can "call into existence" the things that are not. The Lord changed Abram's name to Abraham, which means "Father of a multitude of nations," even before he had Isaac, the heir to the promise (Genesis17:4). The Lord did the same with Sarai his wife; her name was changed to Sarah, "mother of nations," before Isaac was born (v.16). The Lord prophesied over them calling them things that were not as though they were. In Judges 6:12, the Lord called Gideon, who was the least in his family and from the weakest clan in Manasseh, "mighty man of valor," just as he was hiding in fear from the Midianites!

At the weakest moments in our lives we are the strongest because His grace is sufficient for us (2 Corinthians 12:9-10), and when we are weak, we are strong. "Let the weak say, I am a warrior." (Joel 3:10). The Lord changed Simon's name to Peter, which means rock, even though Peter was impulsive, unstable and driven by his emotions. He was many things but (solid) rock! One moment he was inspired by the Holy Spirit, the next moment by the devil. (Matthew 16:13-23). Still, Jesus called him "rock." Isaiah 35:3-4 says "Strengthen the weak hands, and make firm the feeble knees. Say to those who are of a fearful heart, Be strong, fear not!"

In 1 Kings 17, the Lord sends the prophet Elijah during a time of famine to a widow in Sidon, telling him, "Behold, I have commanded a widow there to feed you." When the prophet got there, he asked the widow for water and bread. She answered "As the Lord your God lives, I have nothing baked, only a handful of meal in a jar, and a little oil in a cruse; and now, I am gathering a couple of sticks, that I may go in and prepare it for myself and my son, that we may eat it and die." Here was Elijah, sent by God, to a poor widow who had almost no food; she was ready to die! Did God make a mistake sending the prophet to a poor widow who had only a little food left? No way! Elijah didn't freak out, he didn't grumble and complain at the widow's lack of food, he simply prophesied and called the things that were not as though they were. In verse 14, Elijah tells the widow "For thus says the Lord the God of Israel, the jar of meal shall not be spent, and the cruse of oil shall not fail, until the day that the Lord sends rain upon the earth." And that's exactly what happened. Elijah knew the power in his words as he walked in faith. "Blessed are those who have not seen and yet believe" (John 20:29).

My friend Cristina has a son who was diagnosed with ADD and other learning disabilities; the "experts" told her that her son would never be able to go to a regular high-school and to not even think about sending him to a regular college. My friend interceded day and night for her son, and she called the things that were not as though they were, establishing that her son had "the mind of Christ," that he was the "head and not the tail," that he would be able to take his exams and finish them on time, and whatever else the Holy Spirit led her to prophesy. She laid hands on him, prayed over his pillow, over his clothes, always proclaiming words of life and prophesying the Word of God over her son's life. Not only did he graduate from a regular high-school, but he has just graduated from a regular university. Praise the Lord! The "experts" make great diagnoses; however, we have a God who heals His people! They have their reports, but we choose to believe God's report! Is anything too difficult for our God? Cristina could prophesy life over her son with confidence, because she knew in her heart that the Lord wanted her son healed and made whole. She was the channel that God used to bring life and healing to her son; however, the words and phrases that she used were in one accord with the Lord's. Proverbs 10:11 says that "The mouth of the righteous is a fountain of life…."

During difficult situations that seem to have no way out, ask the Lord what the solution is so that you can pray it. He says "... new things I now declare; before they spring forth I tell you of them" (Isaiah 42:9). He also says in Isaiah 46:10 "declaring the end from the beginning and from ancient times things not yet done, saying, My counsel shall stand, and I will accomplish all my purpose." This means you must spend time in prayer and in the Word so that you are open to His guidance. When you know the end, you will be able to pray prophetically with great success, bringing about God's desired results!

Start prophesying over your lives, your children's future, your business, proclaiming God's blessing and provision over every area of lack and need in your family. Call the things that are not as though they were; remember, we have the power of life and death in our tongues! Get in agreement with the Lord and speak out His Word without reservation! Get rid of the negative statements and fill up with the Word! Take advantage at Mass and proclaim boldly the response to the Psalms and believe what you say with expectant faith! The Lord says that He "confirms the word of his servant, and performs the counsel of his messengers…" (Isaiah 44:26).

AGREE WITH THE LORD!

Hebrews 3:1 "Therefore, holy brethren, who share in a heavenly call, consider Jesus, the apostle and high priest of our confession."

Jesus is the high priest of our confession. Confession of what? Confession of what the Word says. He sits at the right hand of the Father interceding for us. Every promise of God, every promise in the Word is "Yes" and "Amen" in Christ Jesus (2 Corinthians 1:20). Jesus is high priest as we confess His Word. He represents us before the Father; he goes on our behalf with the Word. He is the Word! We must be in agreement with Jesus, just as we must be in agreement with our defense attorney in a court case. Jesus is the high priest of our confession, not our silence; this means that something has to be confessed with our tongues for Him to represent us. He is not the high priest of our negativity, of our grumbling and whining, of our complaining. This means that we need to be determined to walk and talk in agreement with the Lord; as we walk by faith we focus on the Lord and His promises, not on the circumstances. We must grow in our walk with the Lord and not stay all our lives in the infant stages of our spiritual life.

Hebrews 4:4 says to "let us hold fast our confession." This means to hold on to the Word, to the promise we're believing God for. Sometimes we don't see the answer to prayer right away, even though we're praying God's perfect will, which is the Word. In the meantime, we don't waver; we "hold fast" to our confession. In Hebrews 10:23 it says to hold fast to that confession without wavering. I have a lady bulldog and she loves to play with my slippers! She bites into my slippers and she just won't let go! This is how God wants us to be with Him! To not let go when we don't get the answer right away, but to hold on and persevere in prayer until we see it; like Jacob wrestling God. Jacob told the Lord "I will not let you go until you bless me." (Genesis 32:26).

In 1996 I finally went to my native land of Cuba as part of an evangelistic outreach. Since I'm a Cuban-American, and not exactly Castro's favorite kind of people, I asked the Lord for guidance (whether to go or not to go). I really wanted to go to Cuba; but was it God's will? The Lord had told me four years earlier that one day I would go to Cuba to preach the gospel; but was it now God's perfect timing? I prayed and I woke up one morning with Ps. 91:11 "For he will give his angels charge of you to guard you in all your ways." This verse just kept coming and coming at me; I went to noon Mass and it was Psalm 91that was read and the response was verse eleven. I knew then without the shadow of a doubt that it was the Lord speaking to me, reassuring me that I was supposed to go to Cuba! My papers took forever to be approved by the Cuban government, but finally the trip was set for March 1996. Three weeks before the trip, Castro's government shot down two Cuban-American planes from Miami; four Cuban-Americans died! The Cuban community in Miami was outraged and upset! So many people kept telling me that I should cancel the trip to Cuba and not go; many kept asking me "Aren't you afraid?" I WAS NOT AFRAID, THE LORD HAD GIVEN ME HIS WORD, AND I CHOSE TO BELIEVE AND STAND BY IT! Needless to say, I went to Cuba and came back home safely; I was not afraid one bit; after all, the God of the universe had told me that He had given "His angels charge over me, to guard me in all my ways." I stood on that Word fearlessly, and kept claiming it in agreement with the Lord, the High Priest of my confession!

Amos 3:3 says "Do two walk together, unless they have made an appointment?" In the Jewish Bible I like how it is translated: "Do two people travel together without having so agreed?" This means that to walk together with the Lord and get to our destination, we must be in agreement; we must be in one spirit. How can we walk with Jesus in harmony and peace without agreement? How can we reach the place we're supposed to reach without agreement? Of course, we humans must change to agree with Him because God's thoughts are not our thoughts, neither are our ways His ways! (Isaiah 55:8). We must be conformed to the Lord and His Word. Our minds need to be renewed daily with the Word of God so that we start thinking like God thinks for there to be agreement. In other words, we need to be an obedient people, but before we can obey we must know what he desires; we must be "doers of the Word" (James 1:22).

If we want to make it to our destiny and possess the "promised life," remember that we need to take control of our tongue, because our tongue is like the bit in the horse's mouth and the rudder of a ship; depending on how we control our tongue we will or will not make it to our destination. The ten spies that brought the negative report disagreed with God's Word and they never entered the Promised Land. Let's agree with our High Priest who "appears in the presence of God on our behalf." (Hebrews 9:24).

SPEAK TO THE MOUNTAINS!

Mark 11:22-24 "Have faith in God. Truly, I say to you, whoever says to this mountain, Be taken up and cast into the sea, and does not doubt in his heart, but believes that what he says will come to pass, it will be done for him. Therefore I tell you, whatever you ask in prayer, believe that you receive it, and you will."

We see in this passage on faith the importance that Jesus gives to the use of our words. First of all, we need to speak to the mountains, not talk about them all day long! Remember that our words can be a magnet to attract good or evil, and we want to use our tongues to push those mountains out of our lives, rather than establishing them with our tongues. Second of all, we see the connection between our heart and our words. Jesus says that if we believe what we say, it will come to pass. If you're believing His Word, (not what the T.V. says), you will see it come to pass. Stand on the Word, which is solid rock; He says "believe that you receive it, and you will." James says not to doubt, "for he who doubts is like a wave of the sea that is driven and tossed by the wind. For that person must not suppose that a double-minded man, unstable in all his ways, will receive anything from the Lord." (James 1:6-8) An unstable person says one thing now, another thing later; he's driven by his emotions and circumstances and is not anchored in the Word. An unstable person does not walk by faith, but is tossed by the waves of adversity from one frame of mind to another. A stable person, on the other hand, believes God and His promises, stands on the rock of His Word, believing and confessing it, no matter what the circumstance. He knows that His God is bigger than any circumstance; therefore his eyes are fixed on God and not on the problem; he's anchored in the rock of the Word and not tossed by the winds of adversity!

I had a growth on my eye lid that kept growing and looking pretty nasty. I went to the eye doctor and he told me I had an infected gland; it needed to be removed for it was going to get bigger and bigger. Therefore, he told me to come back to have it scraped off my eyelid. He would, of course, give me a shot of anesthesia in my eyelid before scraping it. Afterward, I would have an eye patch for 24 hours. When I got home, I talked to the Lord, my Healer, and I reminded Him that He says in His Word that if we speak to the mountain to be removed and "cast into the sea" without doubting, but believing, "it will be done for him." I told the Lord "this is not even a mountain, but a little growth!" So in the name of Jesus I cursed the root of this growth and commanded it to be gone. It did not disappear right away; as a matter of fact, it grew even more; but I held my ground, walking in faith, proclaiming the Word of the Lord and declaring it out loud. I just thanked God in faith. Within a few weeks it started to become smaller and smaller and within a year it was gone. Personally, I would have desired it to disappear right away, but the Lord is the Healer, not me; it's according to His time table. When we pray for healing according to His Word, He heals; the speed with which He heals and how He will heal is in His hands, not ours; the thing for us to do after we pray for healing, until we see it with our eyes is to thank the Lord and keep standing on His Word, believing and not wavering. Hebrews 6:12 exhorts us not to become "sluggish, but imitators of those who through faith and patience inherit the promises." Amen!

During times of difficulties and crises, surround yourself with people of faith; many inside the Church are like Thomas; they need to see in order to believe; but as God's people we are supposed to believe first, and then we'll see! Jesus Himself had to kick out the unbelievers that were proclaiming words of death in Jairus' house before He could heal his daughter (Mark 5:35-42). In verse 35 we read that some came from Jairus' house with a "negative report", telling Jairus not to bother Jesus anymore since his daughter had died. Jesus told Jairus "Do not fear, only believe." As you live and move in an atmosphere of faith, this will help you not to waver. Remember, faith comes by hearing and hearing the Word of God. (Romans 10:17). (NKJ).

What are the mountains (obstacles) in your life? What are those barriers that hinder your walk with the Lord and prevent you from experiencing the abundant life? Ask the Holy Spirit for revelation and speak to those mountains and get them out of the way. Remember, you must do the speaking! This is not a mental exercise! Rise up in the name of Jesus and with His authority (you are His child) and drive those mountains, those enemies, those hindrances, those insufficiencies out of your life. Jesus said in Matthew 17:20 "...For truly, I say to you, if you have faith as a grain of mustard seed, you will say to this mountain, Move hence to yonder place, and it will move; and nothing will be impossible to you." What a promise!

Isaiah 41:15-16 says "Behold, I will make of you a threshing sledge, new, sharp, and having teeth; you shall thresh the mountains and crush them, and you shall make the hills like chaff; you shall winnow them and the wind shall carry them away, and the tempest shall scatter them. And you shall rejoice in the Lord; in the Holy One of Israel you shall glory." It's God's wish that we experience His power and glory as we cooperate with Him in getting those mountains out of our lives. Use your tongue to see His power and His glory. It's your choice! In the measure that Christ lives within you, you will exercise His power and authority.

ENTER INTO YOUR DESTINY: WORSHIP!

> John 4:23 "But the hour is coming, and now is, when the true worshippers will worship the Father in spirit and truth, for such the Father seeks to worship Him."

The Father is not looking for worship, but for worshippers, people that will worship Him in "spirit and truth." To worship in spirit means that you have to be born again (John 3:3). If you are a child of God, you have been born again. The born again experience becomes real to us when we repent and place our trust for our salvation in the finished work of Jesus at the Cross; when He truly becomes our Lord and Savior. To worship in truth means that we know Jesus, who is the Truth (John 14:6) and His Word. How can we not worship the Lord Jesus once we realize what He has done for us? When we realize that what we deserve is hell, because of sin, but in Him we have received mercy and forgiveness for our sins, and now we are heaven-bound, how can we not adore and worship Him? We are receiving what we don't deserve! Worship then becomes our response to the Lord.

St. Paul says that to present our bodies as living sacrifices is our true spiritual worship. In other words, our entire being, our lives, everything that we are and have, is consecrated to the Lord. (Romans 12:1).

Revelation 4 shows what heaven (our destiny) is like: a 24-hour worship service! Verse eight says that the four living creatures never cease day and night to say "Holy, holy, holy is the Lord God Almighty, who was and is and is to come." In verses ten and eleven, "the twenty-four elders fall down before him who is seated on the throne and worship him who lives for ever and ever; they cast their crowns before the throne, singing, Worthy art thou, our Lord and God, to receive glory and honor and power, for thou didst create all things, and by thy will they existed and were created." We begin to enter into our destiny here as we live a life of praise and worship; when we begin to "cast our crowns" before His throne! Worship becomes our life style when everything that we do, we "do all to the glory of God." (1 Corinthians 10:31).

Mary of Bethany worshipped Jesus by anointing Him with a very costly ointment of pure nard (John 12:1-8). Today we anoint Him with our praises and worship; just as "the house was filled with the fragrance of the ointment," let the earth be filled with "the fragrance of our praises and worship;" and as we do, the atmosphere surrounding us will be changed into a place where the Holy Spirit is welcomed and His presence manifested.

Isaiah was a priest and a prophet; he was a holy man of God. However, something happened to him when he saw a vision of heaven, with the "Lord sitting on a throne, high and lifted up...." (Isaiah 6:1). When he saw the glory, holiness and majesty of God, he could only humble himself before the Lord, realizing his own unworthiness. "Woe is me, for I am lost; for I am a man of unclean lips, and I dwell in the midst of a people of unclean lips..." Isaiah realized that sin permeated his whole being, and it manifested even in his speech. He realized that his tongue needed healing! Then came a seraphim with a burning coal from the altar and "touched my mouth, and said: "Behold, this has touched your lips; your guilt is taken away, and your sin is forgiven." The first thing the seraphim did was to cleanse Isaiah's mouth! Let's cleanse ourselves, tongues and mouths included, with the Blood of Jesus, for we are His Bride and we are to make ourselves "ready!" (Revelation 19:7). The Lord will not come back for a Bride with a foul mouth; He's coming for a Bride that is "without spot or wrinkle or any such thing, that she might be holy and without blemish." (Ephesians 5:27). In the Song of Solomon 4:11, the bridegroom tells the bride: "your lips distil nectar, my bride; honey and milk are under your tongue..." If you love Jesus, isn't it your desire to be beautiful for Him? Is He pleased with your vocabulary, your comments, opinions and remarks? Is the Bridegroom glorified every time you speak?

My dear brothers and sisters, I pray that by now the Holy Spirit has spoken to you personally on the importance of keeping our tongues "tamed." God has given us tremendous power in our tongues; let's become instruments that bring life and not death!

Let's use our tongues to proclaim the Word of God and God's promises; to prophesy and edify and call the things that are not as though they were; to thank and praise the Lord in every circumstance.

It's our choice in this planet to cross from slavery to sin to freedom; from darkness to light; from bondage to deliverance; from depression into the joy of the Lord; from sickness to health; from negativity to right thinking. The victory has been won at Calvary by the Lord Jesus Christ and now it's our choice to enter in! He wants us to experience His abundant life! However, the way that we use our tongue is crucial; depending on how we use our tongues we will, or will not, get to our destiny. This book is not meant to be a "formula," but rather a transforming experience through immersion in the Word of God to help you become the person the Lord created you to be, "holy and blameless before Him." (Ephesians 1:4b).

If Jesus has changed your life, go share the "good news" with others! Don't keep it to yourself, but pass it on! This is really using your tongue for life! Praise the Lord!

PRAYER FOR HEALING

Father, I come boldly before your throne of grace through the Blood of Jesus to ask for healing (Hebrews 4:10). I thank You that on the Cross You made provision for my healing, for Your Word says that You carried every sickness and disease and that by your wounds we are healed (Isaiah 53:4-5; Matthew 8:17; 1 Peter 2:24). I stand on Your Word; I believe Your Word. In faith I receive my healing now, knowing that You are a merciful and compassionate God. I thank You and praise You for You are the God that "forgives all my iniquities and heals all my diseases" (Ps.103:3). I pray in Jesus' name, Amen.

PRAYER TO BREAK WORD CURSES

Lord Jesus I thank You that on the Cross of Calvary you became a curse for me so that I could walk in freedom. (Galatians 3:13). I come against every spoken negative word pronounced over my life or against me, either by myself or someone else. In the name of Jesus and by the power of His Blood, I break and cancel the power of these words and I declare them powerless over my life. I speak a reversal over my life right now. These words have no power over me any longer. I speak and proclaim the blessings of Deuteronomy 28:1-14 over my life. Thank you, Jesus, for setting me free. Amen.